The Complete

FICHAIY

AIR FRYER

COOKBOOK

QUICK AND DELICIOUS RECIPES FOR EVERY DAY INCL.

SIDE DISHES, DESSERTS AND MORE

ROBERT HILL

CONTENTS

INTRODUCTION

Getting to Know the Fichaiy Air Fryer

Deep-frying your food may taste amazing, but it's certainly not beneficial for your health. Air fryers perform convective heat transfer, or convection: A heating element heats the surrounding air and then an internal fan rapidly circulates that heated air. Because the heated air is circulated, it makes contact with every bit of surface area on the food, crisping your food and creating a nice crust without the use of excessive oil and grease. In an air fryer, food typically sits in a perforated basket or on a wire rack inside the air fryer, which also facilitates contact between heated air and every surface of the food.

Seeing the Benefits of the Fichaiy Air Fryer

Healthier Cooking

Air fryers are a great option if you're looking for a healthy alternative to typically fatty foods. With an air fryer, you can cook all your favorite fried dishes without the unhealthy amount of oil present in their deep-fried versions. Air fryers are specifically designed to cook with less oil, producing food with up to 80% less fat than traditional fryers. You can cook without any oil at all, or you can toss your food in a small amount of oil before cooking for an extra crunch.

Quick Meals

Since they're smaller than an oven and circulate air more rapidly, air fryers cook food faster than other appliances. Air fryers can achieve high temperatures within minutes (or seconds), a process that usually takes at least 10 minutes with a traditional oven. An air fryer is a great option for you if you don't have a lot of time to cook meals. However, keep in mind that most air fryers can only cook so fast because of their small size, so if you have a large family, it may be hard for you to cook for everyone at once.

Adaptability

Air fryers are known for their extreme versatility. When we say they can cook almost anything, we mean it. You can cook fresh foods as well as frozen foods and even reheat leftovers. Remember, if you're looking for a frying effect, breaded foods do better than battered foods. Look for different accessories and attachments, such as additional fry baskets, baking racks, and cooking pans, to increase your air fryer's functionality even more!

Easy Cleanup

Cleanup – the dreaded process at the end of cooking. Air fryers make cleaning simpler at the end of meals. Most of their internal components are removable for easy cleaning. For added convenience, many are even dishwasher-safe. Easy cleanup can cut down on the amount of time you spend in the kitchen and encourage you to cook more often.

Tips and Tricks on How to Use the Fichaiy Air Fryer

Don't be intimated by the air fryer! Once you get the hang of it, you'll never know how you lived without it before. Try these tips to cook with your air fryer like a pro:

(1) Always Preheat Before Cooking – Think of your air fryer like a little oven. If yours doesn't have a preheat feature, allow it to warm up for 3-5 minutes before you begin cooking.

(2) Spray the Basket – Even if your recipe doesn't call for oil, be sure to spray the basket's bottom for best results! You can use cooking spray, butter, or grease it with a little olive oil.

(3) Don't Overfill the Basket – Cook in batches if you need to! It's important not to let your food overlap. If you try to squeeze too much in, you may end up with a soggy, undercooked mess. Easy does it!

(4) Flip or Shake Foods You Want Crispy – If you're cooking french fries or chicken wings, flip them halfway through or remove the basket and shake. This helps them crisp evenly.

(5) Invest in Baking Pans & Accessories – These air fryer accessories will make life so much easier and cleaning a breeze!

(6) Have Fun & Experiment – We think this tip is the most important! Once you get the hang of cooking with your air fryer, have some fun with it. Branch out and try new things! You'll get used to the cooking times, breading methods, and more, so use your knowledge to create new recipes.

Hints on Cleaning the Fichaiy Air Fryer

Cleaning and preserving are the most important factors to decide the durability of an appliance. The best time to clean an air fryer is immediately after use, which will ensure that food particles do not stick to the sides and become hard to remove. However, do not rush and let the machine cool down about 30 minutes before cleaning. Air fryers usually come with an instruction manual; hence, you can also refer to this manual to see how best you can care for your new device to extend the useful lifespan saving you money in the long term.

◆ Clean the frying basket

1) The bottom frying basket is where lots of grease and gunk falls, so cleaning it properly to prevent grease build-up and bacteria growth that could foul the foods and make you sick. You can proceed to clean the basket according to the following instructions:

2) Make sure that the device is unplugged from the power source and wait until it's cool to start cleaning. You can remove the air fryer basket and either set it in the sink or on the counter. This will help it cool down even faster.

3) Use a damp cloth to wipe down the exterior. Wipe away the soap with a clean damp cloth. And repeat this step for the interior.

4) Remove the basket and tray from the main unit, then use a bit of dish soap with warm water to wash them with a soft sponge or cloth—no abrasives.

5) If food is stuck on these components, you should soak them in hot soapy water for at least 10 minutes before scrubbing with a non-abrasive sponge.

6) Don't forget to dry it completely before you put it back in the air fryer!

7) It's a good idea to clean the frying basket after each use to ensure to remove all old foods and grease causes to smell and effects to the taste of food.

◆ Clean the Crumb Basket

1) Take the crumb basket out and throw away any loose pieces of food leftover in it. Wipe it out with a damp cloth.
2) Make sure you clean all the crevices and both the outside and inside of the basket. It might help to use a dish brush or toothbrush to clean all the slats.
3) Dry it completely. Make sure it completely dry before replacing them in the air fryer.

Note:

➢ The crumb basket has a non-stick coating on it, so please don't use abrasive brushes (like steel wool) on it or any abrasive cleaners that might erode this coating. This is why we do not recommend using a dishwasher. They operate at high heat which erodes the surface of the nonstick cookware. It can lead to flaking which can be toxic.
➢ We are also against using any strong detergents or things that aren't designed to clean. Often, these can have the opposite effect and actually cause damage instead of cleaning.

BREAD AND BREAKFAST

Strawberry Streusel Muffins

Servings: 12   Cooking Time: 14 Minutes

Ingredients:

- 1¾ cups all-purpose flour
- ½ cup granulated sugar
- 2 teaspoons baking powder
- ¼ teaspoon baking soda
- ½ teaspoon salt
- ½ cup plain yogurt
- ½ cup milk
- ¼ cup vegetable oil
- 2 large eggs
- 1 teaspoon vanilla extract
- ½ cup freeze-dried strawberries
- 2 tablespoons brown sugar
- ¼ cup oats
- 2 tablespoons butter

Directions:

1. Preheat the air fryer to 330°F.

2. In a large bowl, whisk together the flour, sugar, baking powder, baking soda, and salt; set aside.

3. In a separate bowl, whisk together the yogurt, milk, vegetable oil, eggs, and vanilla extract.

4. Make a well in the dry ingredients; then pour the wet ingredients into the well of the dry ingredients. Using a rubber spatula, mix the ingredients for 1 minute or until slightly lumpy. Fold in the strawberries.

5. In a small bowl, use your fingers to mix together the brown sugar, oats, and butter until coarse crumbles appear. Divide the mixture in half.

6. Using silicone muffin liners, fill 6 muffin liners two-thirds full.

7. Crumble half of the streusel topping onto the first batch of muffins.

8. Carefully place the muffin liners in the air fryer basket and bake for 14 minutes (or until the tops are browned and a toothpick inserted in the center comes out clean). Carefully remove the muffins from the basket and repeat with the remaining batter and topping.

9. Serve warm.

Hole In One

Servings: 1

Cooking Time: 7 Minutes

Ingredients:

- 1 slice bread
- 1 teaspoon soft butter
- 1 egg
- salt and pepper
- 1 tablespoon shredded Cheddar cheese
- 2 teaspoons diced ham

Directions:

1. Place a 6 x 6-inch baking dish inside air fryer basket and preheat fryer to 330°F.
2. Using a 2½-inch-diameter biscuit cutter, cut a hole in center of bread slice.
3. Spread softened butter on both sides of bread.
4. Lay bread slice in baking dish and crack egg into the hole. Sprinkle egg with salt and pepper to taste.
5. Cook for 5minutes.
6. Turn toast over and top it with shredded cheese and diced ham.
7. Cook for 2 more minutes or until yolk is done to your liking.

Christmas Eggnog Bread

Servings: 6

Cooking Time: 18 Minutes

Ingredients:

- 1 cup flour, plus more for dusting
- ¼ cup sugar
- 1 teaspoon baking powder
- ¼ teaspoon salt
- ¼ teaspoon nutmeg
- ½ cup eggnog
- 1 egg yolk
- 1 tablespoon butter, plus 1 teaspoon, melted
- ¼ cup pecans
- ¼ cup chopped candied fruit (cherries, pineapple, or mixed fruits)
- cooking spray

Directions:

1. Preheat air fryer to 360°F.
2. In a medium bowl, stir together the flour, sugar, baking powder, salt, and nutmeg.
3. Add eggnog, egg yolk, and butter. Mix well but do not beat.
4. Stir in nuts and fruit.
5. Spray a 6 x 6-inch baking pan with cooking spray and dust with flour.
6. Spread batter into prepared pan and cook at 360°F for 18 minutes or until top is dark golden brown and bread starts to pull away from sides of pan.

Country Gravy

Servings: 2

Cooking Time: 7 Minutes

Ingredients:

- ¼ pound pork sausage, casings removed
- 1 tablespoon butter
- 2 tablespoons flour
- 2 cups whole milk
- ½ teaspoon salt
- freshly ground black pepper
- 1 teaspoon fresh thyme leaves

Directions:

1. Preheat a saucepan over medium heat. Add and brown the sausage, crumbling it into small pieces as it cooks. Add the butter and flour, stirring well to combine. Continue to cook for 2 minutes, stirring constantly.

2. Slowly pour in the milk, whisking as you do, and bring the mixture to a boil to thicken. Season with salt and freshly ground black pepper, lower the heat and simmer until the sauce has thickened to your desired consistency – about 5 minutes. Stir in the fresh thyme, season to taste and serve hot.

Roasted Tomato And Cheddar Rolls

Servings: 12

Cooking Time: 55 Minutes

Ingredients:

- 4 Roma tomatoes
- ½ clove garlic, minced
- 1 tablespoon olive oil
- ¼ teaspoon dried thyme
- salt and freshly ground black pepper
- 4 cups all-purpose flour
- 1 teaspoon active dry yeast
- 2 teaspoons sugar
- 2 teaspoons salt
- 1 tablespoon olive oil
- 1 cup grated Cheddar cheese, plus more for sprinkling at the end
- 1½ cups water

Directions:

1. Cut the Roma tomatoes in half, remove the seeds with your fingers and transfer to a bowl. Add the garlic, olive oil, dried thyme, salt and freshly ground black pepper and toss well.

2. Preheat the air fryer to 390°F.

3. Place the tomatoes, cut side up in the air fryer basket and air-fry for 10 minutes. The tomatoes should just start to brown. Shake the basket to redistribute the tomatoes, and air-fry for another 5 to 10 minutes at 330°F until the tomatoes are no longer juicy. Let the tomatoes cool and then rough chop them.

4. Combine the flour, yeast, sugar and salt in the bowl of a stand mixer. Add the olive oil, chopped roasted tomatoes and Cheddar cheese to the flour mixture and start to mix using the dough hook attachment. As you're mixing, add 1¼ cups of the water, mixing until the dough comes together. Continue to knead the dough with the dough hook for another 10 minutes, adding enough water to the dough to get it to the right consistency.

5. Transfer the dough to an oiled bowl, cover with a clean kitchen towel and let it rest and rise until it has doubled in volume – about 1 to 2 hours. Then, divide the dough into 12 equal portions. Roll each portion of dough into a ball. Lightly coat each dough ball with oil and let the dough balls rest and rise a second time, covered lightly with plastic wrap for 45 minutes. (Alternately, you can place the rolls in the refrigerator overnight and take them out 2 hours before you bake them.)

6. Preheat the air fryer to 360°F.

7. Spray the dough balls and the air fryer basket with a little olive oil. Place three rolls at a time in the basket and bake for 10 minutes. Add a little grated Cheddar cheese on top of the rolls for the last 2 minutes of air frying for an attractive finish.

Quiche Cups

Servings: 10

Cooking Time: 16 Minutes

Ingredients:

- ¼ pound all-natural ground pork sausage
- 3 eggs
- ¾ cup milk
- 20 foil muffin cups
- cooking spray
- 4 ounces sharp Cheddar cheese, grated

Directions:

1. Divide sausage into 3 portions and shape each into a thin patty.
2. Place patties in air fryer basket and cook 390°F for 6minutes.
3. While sausage is cooking, prepare the egg mixture. A large measuring cup or bowl with a pouring lip works best. Combine the eggs and milk and whisk until well blended. Set aside.
4. When sausage has cooked fully, remove patties from basket, drain well, and use a fork to crumble the meat into small pieces.
5. Double the foil cups into 10 sets. Remove paper liners from the top muffin cups and spray the foil cups lightly with cooking spray.
6. Divide crumbled sausage among the 10 muffin cup sets.
7. Top each with grated cheese, divided evenly among the cups.
8. Place 5 cups in air fryer basket.
9. Pour egg mixture into each cup, filling until each cup is at least ⅔ full.
10. Cook for 8 minutes and test for doneness. A knife inserted into the center shouldn't have any raw egg on it when removed.
11. If needed, cook 2 more minutes, until egg completely sets.
12. Repeat steps 8 through 11 for the remaining quiches.

Hashbrown Potatoes Lyonnaise

Servings: 4

Cooking Time: 33 Minutes

Ingredients:

- 1 Vidalia (or other sweet) onion, sliced
- 1 teaspoon butter, melted
- 1 teaspoon brown sugar
- 2 large russet potatoes (about 1 pound), sliced ½-inch thick
- 1 tablespoon vegetable oil
- salt and freshly ground black pepper

Directions:

1. Preheat the air fryer to 370°F.

2. Toss the sliced onions, melted butter and brown sugar together in the air fryer basket. Air-fry for 8 minutes, shaking the basket occasionally to help the onions cook evenly.

3. While the onions are cooking, bring a 3-quart saucepan of salted water to a boil on the stovetop. Par-cook the potatoes in boiling water for 3 minutes. Drain the potatoes and pat them dry with a clean kitchen towel.

4. Add the potatoes to the onions in the air fryer basket and drizzle with vegetable oil. Toss to coat the potatoes with the oil and season with salt and freshly ground black pepper.

5. Increase the air fryer temperature to 400°F and air-fry for 22 minutes tossing the vegetables a few times during the cooking time to help the potatoes brown evenly. Season to taste again with salt and freshly ground black pepper and serve warm.

Cheesy Olive And Roasted Pepper Bread

Servings: 8

Cooking Time: 7 Minutes

Ingredients:

- 7-inch round bread boule
- olive oil
- ½ cup mayonnaise
- 2 tablespoons butter, melted
- 1 cup grated mozzarella or Fontina cheese
- ¼ cup grated Parmesan cheese
- ½ teaspoon dried oregano
- ½ cup black olives, sliced
- ½ cup green olives, sliced
- ½ cup coarsely chopped roasted red peppers
- 2 tablespoons minced red onion
- freshly ground black pepper

Directions:

1. Preheat the air fryer to 370°F.

2. Cut the bread boule in half horizontally. If your bread boule has a rounded top, trim the top of the boule so that the top half will lie flat with the cut side facing up. Lightly brush both sides of the boule halves with olive oil.

3. Place one half of the boule into the air fryer basket with the center cut side facing down. Air-fry at 370°F for 2 minutes to lightly toast the bread. Repeat with the other half of the bread boule.

4. Combine the mayonnaise, butter, mozzarella cheese, Parmesan cheese and dried oregano in a small bowl. Fold in the black and green olives, roasted red peppers and red onion and season with freshly ground black pepper. Spread the cheese mixture over the untoasted side of the bread, covering the entire surface.

5. Air-fry at 350°F for 5 minutes until the cheese is melted and browned. Repeat with the other half. Cut into slices and serve warm.

Soft Pretzels

Servings: 12

Cooking Time: 6 Minutes

Ingredients:

- 2 teaspoons yeast
- 1 cup water, warm
- 1 teaspoon sugar
- 1 teaspoon salt
- 2½ cups all-purpose flour

- 2 tablespoons butter, melted
- 1 cup boiling water
- 1 tablespoon baking soda
- coarse sea salt
- melted butter

Directions:

1. Combine the yeast and water in a small bowl. Combine the sugar, salt and flour in the bowl of a stand mixer. With the mixer running and using the dough hook, drizzle in the yeast mixture and melted butter and knead dough until smooth and elastic – about 10 minutes. Shape into a ball and let the dough rise for 1 hour.

2. Punch the dough down to release any air and decide what size pretzels you want to make.

3. a. To make large pretzels, divide the dough into 12 portions.

4. b. To make medium sized pretzels, divide the dough into 24 portions.

5. c. To make mini pretzel knots, divide the dough into 48 portions.

6. Roll each portion into a skinny rope using both hands on the counter and rolling from the center to the ends of the rope. Spin the rope into a pretzel shape (or tie the rope into a knot) and place the tied pretzels on a parchment lined baking sheet.

7. Preheat the air fryer to 350°F.

8. Combine the boiling water and baking soda in a shallow bowl and whisk to dissolve (this mixture will bubble, but it will settle down). Let the water cool so that you can put your hands in it. Working in batches, dip the pretzels (top side down) into the baking soda-water mixture and let them soak for 30 seconds to a minute. (This step is what gives pretzels their texture and helps them to brown faster.) Then, remove the pretzels carefully and return them (top side up) to the baking sheet. Sprinkle the coarse salt on the top.

9. Air-fry in batches for 3 minutes per side. When the pretzels are finished, brush them generously with the melted butter and enjoy them warm with some spicy mustard.

POULTRY RECIPES

Sweet Chili Spiced Chicken

Servings: 4

Cooking Time: 43 Minutes

Ingredients:

- Spice Rub:
- 2 tablespoons brown sugar
- 2 tablespoons paprika
- 1 teaspoon dry mustard powder
- 1 teaspoon chili powder
- 2 tablespoons coarse sea salt or kosher salt
- 2 teaspoons coarsely ground black pepper
- 1 tablespoon vegetable oil
- 1 (3½-pound) chicken, cut into 8 pieces

Directions:

1. Prepare the spice rub by combining the brown sugar, paprika, mustard powder, chili powder, salt and pepper. Rub the oil all over the chicken pieces and then rub the spice mix onto the chicken, covering completely. This is done very easily in a zipper sealable bag. You can do this ahead of time and let the chicken marinate in the refrigerator, or just proceed with cooking right away.

2. Preheat the air fryer to 370°F.

3. Air-fry the chicken in two batches. Place the two chicken thighs and two drumsticks into the air fryer basket. Air-fry at 370°F for 10 minutes. Then, gently turn the chicken pieces over and air-fry for another 10 minutes. Remove the chicken pieces and let them rest on a plate while you cook the chicken breasts. Air-fry the chicken breasts, skin side down for 8 minutes. Turn the chicken breasts over and air-fry for another 12 minutes.

4. Lower the temperature of the air fryer to 340°F. Place the first batch of chicken on top of the second batch already in the basket and air-fry for a final 3 minutes.

5. Let the chicken rest for 5 minutes and serve warm with some mashed potatoes and a green salad or vegetables.

Coconut Curry Chicken With Coconut Rice

Servings: 4

Cooking Time: 56 Minutes

Ingredients:

- 1 (14-ounce) can coconut milk
- 2 tablespoons green or red curry paste
- zest and juice of one lime
- 1 clove garlic, minced
- 1 tablespoon grated fresh ginger
- 1 teaspoon ground cumin
- 1 (3- to 4-pound) chicken, cut into 8 pieces
- vegetable or olive oil
- salt and freshly ground black pepper
- fresh cilantro leaves
- For the rice:
- 1 cup basmati or jasmine rice
- 1 cup water
- 1 cup coconut milk
- ½ teaspoon salt
- freshly ground black pepper

Directions:

1. Make the marinade by combining the coconut milk, curry paste, lime zest and juice, garlic, ginger and cumin. Coat the chicken on all sides with the marinade and marinate the chicken for 1 hour to overnight in the refrigerator.

2. Preheat the air fryer to 380°F.

3. Brush the bottom of the air fryer basket with oil. Transfer the chicken thighs and drumsticks from the marinade to the air fryer basket, letting most of the marinade drip off. Season to taste with salt and freshly ground black pepper.

4. Air-fry the chicken drumsticks and thighs at 380°F for 12 minutes. Flip the chicken over and continue to air-fry for another 12 minutes. Set aside and air-fry the chicken breast pieces at 380°F for 15 minutes. Turn the chicken breast pieces over and air-fry for another 12 minutes. Return the chicken thighs and drumsticks to the air fryer and air-fry for an additional 5 minutes.

5. While the chicken is cooking, make the coconut rice. Rinse the rice kernels with water and drain well. Place the rice in a medium saucepan with a tight fitting lid, along with the water, coconut milk, salt and freshly ground black pepper. Bring the mixture to a boil and then cover, reduce the heat and let it cook gently for 20 minutes without lifting the lid. When the time is up, lift the lid, fluff with a fork and set aside.

6. Remove the chicken from the air fryer and serve warm with the coconut rice and fresh cilantro scattered around.

Chicken Nuggets

Servings: 20

Cooking Time: 14 Minutes Per Batch

Ingredients:

- 1 pound boneless, skinless chicken thighs, cut into 1-inch chunks
- ¾ teaspoon salt
- ½ teaspoon black pepper
- ½ teaspoon garlic powder
- ½ teaspoon onion powder
- ½ cup flour
- 2 eggs, beaten
- ½ cup panko breadcrumbs
- 3 tablespoons plain breadcrumbs
- oil for misting or cooking spray

Directions:

1. In the bowl of a food processor, combine chicken, ½ teaspoon salt, pepper, garlic powder, and onion powder. Process in short pulses until chicken is very finely chopped and well blended.

2. Place flour in one shallow dish and beaten eggs in another. In a third dish or plastic bag, mix together the panko crumbs, plain breadcrumbs, and ¼ teaspoon salt.

3. Shape chicken mixture into small nuggets. Dip nuggets in flour, then eggs, then panko crumb mixture.

4. Spray nuggets on both sides with oil or cooking spray and place in air fryer basket in a single layer, close but not overlapping.

5. Cook at 360°F for 10minutes. Spray with oil and cook 4 minutes, until chicken is done and coating is golden brown.

6. Repeat step 5 to cook remaining nuggets.

Turkey-hummus Wraps

Servings: 4

Cooking Time: 7 Minutes Per Batch

Ingredients:

- ➢ 4 large whole wheat wraps
- ➢ ½ cup hummus
- ➢ 16 thin slices deli turkey
- ➢ 8 slices provolone cheese
- ➢ 1 cup fresh baby spinach (or more to taste)

Directions:

1. To assemble, place 2 tablespoons of hummus on each wrap and spread to within about a half inch from edges. Top with 4 slices of turkey and 2 slices of provolone. Finish with ¼ cup of baby spinach—or pile on as much as you like.
2. Roll up each wrap. You don't need to fold or seal the ends.
3. Place 2 wraps in air fryer basket, seam side down.
4. Cook at 360°F for 4minutes to warm filling and melt cheese. If you like, you can continue cooking for 3 more minutes, until the wrap is slightly crispy.
5. Repeat step 4 to cook remaining wraps.

Apricot Glazed Chicken Thighs

Servings: 2

Cooking Time: 22 Minutes

Ingredients:

➢ 4 bone-in chicken thighs (about 2 pounds)

➢ olive oil

➢ 1 teaspoon salt

➢ ¼ teaspoon freshly ground black pepper

➢ ½ teaspoon onion powder

➢ ¾ cup apricot preserves 1½ tablespoons Dijon mustard

➢ ½ teaspoon dried thyme

➢ 1 teaspoon soy sauce

➢ fresh thyme leaves, for garnish

Directions:

1. Preheat the air fryer to 380°F.

2. Brush or spray both the air fryer basket and the chicken with the olive oil. Combine the salt, pepper and onion powder and season both sides of the chicken with the spice mixture.

3. Place the seasoned chicken thighs, skin side down in the air fryer basket. Air-fry for 10 minutes.

4. While chicken is cooking, make the glaze by combining the apricot preserves, Dijon mustard, thyme and soy sauce in a small bowl.

5. When the time is up on the air fryer, spoon half of the apricot glaze over the chicken thighs and air-fry for 2 minutes. Then flip the chicken thighs over so that the skin side is facing up and air-fry for an additional 8 minutes. Finally, spoon and spread the rest of the glaze evenly over the chicken thighs and air-fry for a final 2 minutes. Transfer the chicken to a serving platter and sprinkle the fresh thyme leaves on top.

Jerk Chicken Drumsticks

Servings: 2

Cooking Time: 20 Minutes

Ingredients:

- 1 or 2 cloves garlic
- 1 inch of fresh ginger
- 2 serrano peppers, (with seeds if you like it spicy, seeds removed for less heat)
- 1 teaspoon ground allspice
- 1 teaspoon ground nutmeg
- 1 teaspoon chili powder
- ½ teaspoon dried thyme
- ½ teaspoon ground cinnamon
- ½ teaspoon paprika
- 1 tablespoon brown sugar
- 1 teaspoon soy sauce
- 2 tablespoons vegetable oil
- 6 skinless chicken drumsticks

Directions:

1. Combine all the ingredients except the chicken in a small chopper or blender and blend to a paste. Make slashes into the meat of the chicken drumsticks and rub the spice blend all over the chicken (a pair of plastic gloves makes this really easy). Transfer the rubbed chicken to a non-reactive covered container and let the chicken marinate for at least 30 minutes or overnight in the refrigerator.

2. Preheat the air fryer to 400°F.

3. Transfer the drumsticks to the air fryer basket. Air-fry for 10 minutes. Turn the drumsticks over and air-fry for another 10 minutes. Serve warm with some rice and vegetables or a green salad.

Buffalo Egg Rolls

Servings: 8   Cooking Time: 9 Minutes Per Batch

Ingredients:

- 1 teaspoon water
- 1 tablespoon cornstarch
- 1 egg
- 2½ cups cooked chicken, diced or shredded (see opposite page)
- ⅓ cup chopped green onion
- ⅓ cup diced celery
- ⅓ cup buffalo wing sauce
- 8 egg roll wraps
- oil for misting or cooking spray
- Blue Cheese Dip
- 3 ounces cream cheese, softened
- ⅓ cup blue cheese, crumbled
- 1 teaspoon Worcestershire sauce
- ¼ teaspoon garlic powder
- ¼ cup buttermilk (or sour cream)

Directions:

1. Mix water and cornstarch in a small bowl until dissolved. Add egg, beat well, and set aside.
2. In a medium size bowl, mix together chicken, green onion, celery, and buffalo wing sauce.
3. Divide chicken mixture evenly among 8 egg roll wraps, spooning ½ inch from one edge.
4. Moisten all edges of each wrap with beaten egg wash.
5. Fold the short ends over filling, then roll up tightly and press to seal edges.
6. Brush outside of wraps with egg wash, then spritz with oil or cooking spray.
7. Place 4 egg rolls in air fryer basket.
8. Cook at 390°F for 9minutes or until outside is brown and crispy.
9. While the rolls are cooking, prepare the Blue Cheese Dip. With a fork, mash together cream cheese and blue cheese.
10. Stir in remaining ingredients.
11. Dip should be just thick enough to slightly cling to egg rolls. If too thick, stir in buttermilk or milk 1 tablespoon at a time until you reach the desired consistency.
12. Cook remaining 4 egg rolls as in steps 7 and 8.
13. Serve while hot with Blue Cheese Dip, more buffalo wing sauce, or both.

Chicken Hand Pies

Servings: 8

Cooking Time: 10 Minutes Per Batch

Ingredients:

- ¾ cup chicken broth
- ¾ cup frozen mixed peas and carrots
- 1 cup cooked chicken, chopped
- 1 tablespoon cornstarch
- 1 tablespoon milk
- salt and pepper
- 1 8-count can organic flaky biscuits
- oil for misting or cooking spray

Directions:

1. In a medium saucepan, bring chicken broth to a boil. Stir in the frozen peas and carrots and cook for 5minutes over medium heat. Stir in chicken.

2. Mix the cornstarch into the milk until it dissolves. Stir it into the simmering chicken broth mixture and cook just until thickened.

3. Remove from heat, add salt and pepper to taste, and let cool slightly.

4. Lay biscuits out on wax paper. Peel each biscuit apart in the middle to make 2 rounds so you have 16 rounds total. Using your hands or a rolling pin, flatten each biscuit round slightly to make it larger and thinner.

5. Divide chicken filling among 8 of the biscuit rounds. Place remaining biscuit rounds on top and press edges all around. Use the tines of a fork to crimp biscuit edges and make sure they are sealed well.

6. Spray both sides lightly with oil or cooking spray.

7. Cook in a single layer, 4 at a time, at 330°F for 10minutes or until biscuit dough is cooked through and golden brown.

Tandoori Chicken Legs

Servings: 2

Cooking Time: 30 Minutes

Ingredients:

- ➢ 1 cup plain yogurt
- ➢ 2 cloves garlic, minced
- ➢ 1 tablespoon grated fresh ginger
- ➢ 2 teaspoons paprika
- ➢ 2 teaspoons ground coriander
- ➢ 1 teaspoon ground turmeric
- ➢ 1 teaspoon salt
- ➢ ¼ teaspoon ground cayenne pepper
- ➢ juice of 1 lime
- ➢ 2 bone-in, skin-on chicken legs
- ➢ fresh cilantro leaves

Directions:

1. Make the marinade by combining the yogurt, garlic, ginger, spices and lime juice. Make slashes into the chicken legs to help the marinade penetrate the meat. Pour the marinade over the chicken legs, cover and let the chicken marinate for at least an hour or overnight in the refrigerator.

2. Preheat the air fryer to 380°F.

3. Transfer the chicken legs from the marinade to the air fryer basket, reserving any extra marinade. Air-fry for 15 minutes. Flip the chicken over and pour the remaining marinade over the top. Air-fry for another 15 minutes, watching to make sure it doesn't brown too much. If it does start to get too brown, you can loosely tent the chicken with aluminum foil, tucking the ends of the foil under the chicken to stop it from blowing around.

4. Serve over rice with some fresh cilantro on top.

Chicken Strips

Servings: 4

Cooking Time: 8 Minutes

Ingredients:

- 1 pound chicken tenders
- Marinade
- ¼ cup olive oil
- 2 tablespoons water
- 2 tablespoons honey
- 2 tablespoons white vinegar
- ½ teaspoon salt
- ½ teaspoon crushed red pepper
- 1 teaspoon garlic powder
- 1 teaspoon onion powder
- ½ teaspoon paprika

Directions:

1. Combine all marinade ingredients and mix well.
2. Add chicken and stir to coat. Cover tightly and let marinate in refrigerator for 30minutes.
3. Remove tenders from marinade and place them in a single layer in the air fryer basket.
4. Cook at 390°F for 3minutes. Turn tenders over and cook for 5 minutes longer or until chicken is done and juices run clear.
5. Repeat step 4 to cook remaining tenders.

Parmesan Crusted Chicken Cordon Bleu

Servings: 2   Cooking Time: 14 Minutes

Ingredients:

- 2 (6-ounce) boneless, skinless chicken breasts
- salt and freshly ground black pepper
- 1 tablespoon Dijon mustard
- 4 slices Swiss cheese
- 4 slices deli-sliced ham
- ¼ cup all-purpose flour*
- 1 egg, beaten
- ¾ cup panko breadcrumbs*
- ⅓ cup grated Parmesan cheese
- olive oil, in a spray bottle

Directions:

1. Butterfly the chicken breasts. Place the chicken breast on a cutting board and press down on the breast with the palm of your hand. Slice into the long side of the chicken breast, parallel to the cutting board, but not all the way through to the other side. Open the chicken breast like a "book". Place a piece of plastic wrap over the chicken breast and gently pound it with a meat mallet to make it evenly thick.

2. Season the chicken with salt and pepper. Spread the Dijon mustard on the inside of each chicken breast. Layer one slice of cheese on top of the mustard, then top with the 2 slices of ham and the other slice of cheese.

3. Starting with the long edge of the chicken breast, roll the chicken up to the other side. Secure it shut with 1 or 2 toothpicks.

4. Preheat the air fryer to 350°F.

5. Set up a dredging station with three shallow dishes. Place the flour in the first dish. Place the beaten egg in the second shallow dish. Combine the panko breadcrumbs and Parmesan cheese together in the third shallow dish. Dip the stuffed and rolled chicken breasts in the flour, then the beaten egg and then roll in the breadcrumb-cheese mixture to cover on all sides. Press the crumbs onto the chicken breasts with your hands to make sure they are well adhered. Spray the chicken breasts with olive oil and transfer to the air fryer basket.

6. Air-fry at 350°F for 14 minutes, flipping the breasts over halfway through the cooking time. Let the chicken rest for a few minutes before removing the toothpicks, slicing and serving.

Chicken Cutlets With Broccoli Rabe And Roasted Peppers

Servings: 2

Cooking Time: 10 Minutes

Ingredients:

➢ ½ bunch broccoli rabe

➢ olive oil, in a spray bottle

➢ salt and freshly ground black pepper

➢ ⅔ cup roasted red pepper strips

➢ 2 (4-ounce) boneless, skinless chicken breasts

➢ 2 tablespoons all-purpose flour*

➢ 1 egg, beaten

➢ ⅓ cup seasoned breadcrumbs*

➢ 2 slices aged provolone cheese

Directions:

1. Bring a medium saucepot of salted water to a boil on the stovetop. Blanch the broccoli rabe for 3 minutes in the boiling water and then drain. When it has cooled a little, squeeze out as much water as possible, drizzle a little olive oil on top, season with salt and black pepper and set aside. Dry the roasted red peppers with a clean kitchen towel and set them aside as well.

2. Place each chicken breast between 2 pieces of plastic wrap. Use a meat pounder to flatten the chicken breasts to about ½-inch thick. Season the chicken on both sides with salt and pepper.

3. Preheat the air fryer to 400°F.

4. Set up a dredging station with three shallow dishes. Place the flour in one dish, the egg in a second dish and the breadcrumbs in a third dish. Coat the chicken on all sides with the flour. Shake off any excess flour and dip the chicken into the egg. Let the excess egg drip off and coat both sides of the chicken in the breadcrumbs. Spray the chicken with olive oil on both sides and transfer to the air fryer basket.

5. Air-fry the chicken at 400°F for 5 minutes. Turn the chicken over and air-fry for another minute. Then, top the chicken breast with the broccoli rabe and roasted peppers. Place a slice of the provolone cheese on top and secure it with a toothpick or two.

6. Air-fry at 360° for 3 to 4 minutes to melt the cheese and warm everything together.

APPETIZERS AND SNACKS

Smoked Whitefish Spread

Servings: 1   Cooking Time: 10 Minutes

Ingredients:

- ➤ ¾ pound Boneless skinless white-flesh fish fillets, such as hake or trout
- ➤ 3 tablespoons Liquid smoke
- ➤ 3 tablespoons Regular, low-fat, or fat-free mayonnaise (gluten-free, if a concern)

- ➤ 2 teaspoons Jarred prepared white horseradish (optional)
- ➤ ¼ teaspoon Onion powder
- ➤ ¼ teaspoon Celery seeds
- ➤ ¼ teaspoon Table salt
- ➤ ¼ teaspoon Ground black pepper

Directions:

1. Put the fish fillets in a zip-closed bag, add the liquid smoke, and seal closed. Rub the liquid smoke all over the fish , then refrigerate the sealed bag for 2 hours.

2. Preheat the air fryer to 400°F.

3. Set a 12-inch piece of aluminum foil on your work surface. Remove the fish fillets from the bag and set them in the center of this piece of foil (the fillets can overlap). Fold the long sides of the foil together and crimp them closed. Make a tight seam so no steam can escape. Fold up the ends and crimp to seal well.

4. Set the packet in the basket and air-fry undisturbed for 10 minutes.

5. Use kitchen tongs to transfer the foil packet to a wire rack. Cool for a minute or so. Open the packet, transfer the fish to a plate, and refrigerate for 30 minutes.

6. Put the cold fish in a food processor. Add the mayonnaise, horseradish (if using), onion powder, celery seeds, salt, and pepper. Cover and pulse to a slightly coarse spread, certainly not fully smooth.

7. For a more traditional texture, put the fish fillets in a bowl, add the other ingredients, and stir with a wooden spoon, mashing the fish with everything else to make a coarse paste.

8. Scrape the spread into a bowl and serve at once, or cover with plastic wrap and store in the fridge for up to 4 days.

Rumaki

Servings: 24

Cooking Time: 12 Minutes

Ingredients:

- 10 ounces raw chicken livers
- 1 can sliced water chestnuts, drained
- ¼ cup low-sodium teriyaki sauce
- 12 slices turkey bacon
- toothpicks

Directions:

1. Cut livers into 1½-inch pieces, trimming out tough veins as you slice.
2. Place livers, water chestnuts, and teriyaki sauce in small container with lid. If needed, add another tablespoon of teriyaki sauce to make sure livers are covered. Refrigerate for 1 hour.
3. When ready to cook, cut bacon slices in half crosswise.
4. Wrap 1 piece of liver and 1 slice of water chestnut in each bacon strip. Secure with toothpick.
5. When you have wrapped half of the livers, place them in the air fryer basket in a single layer.
6. Cook at 390°F for 12 minutes, until liver is done and bacon is crispy.
7. While first batch cooks, wrap the remaining livers. Repeat step 6 to cook your second batch.

Crunchy Spicy Chickpeas

Servings: 6

Cooking Time: 12 Minutes

Ingredients:

- ➤ 2½ cups Canned chickpeas, drained and rinsed
- ➤ 2½ tablespoons Vegetable or canola oil
- ➤ up to 1 tablespoon Cajun or jerk dried seasoning blend (see here for a Cajun blend, here for a jerk blend)
- ➤ up to ¾ teaspoon Table salt (optional)

Directions:

1. Preheat the air fryer to 400°F.

2. Toss the chickpeas, oil, seasoning blend, and salt (if using) in a large bowl until the chickpeas are evenly coated.

3. When the machine is at temperature, pour the chickpeas into the basket. Air-fry for 12 minutes, removing the basket at the 4- and 8-minute marks to toss and rearrange the chickpeas, until very aromatic and perhaps sizzling but not burned.

4. Pour the chickpeas into a large serving bowl. Cool for a couple of minutes, gently stirring once, before you dive in.

Bacon-wrapped Goat Cheese Poppers

Servings: 10

Cooking Time: 10 Minutes

Ingredients:

➢ 10 large jalapeño peppers

➢ 8 ounces goat cheese

➢ 10 slices bacon

Directions:

1. Preheat the air fryer to 380°F.

2. Slice the jalapeños in half. Carefully remove the veins and seeds of the jalapeños with a spoon.

3. Fill each jalapeño half with 2 teaspoons goat cheese.

4. Cut the bacon in half lengthwise to make long strips. Wrap the jalapeños with bacon, trying to cover the entire length of the jalapeño.

5. Place the bacon-wrapped jalapeños into the air fryer basket. Cook the stuffed jalapeños for 10 minutes or until bacon is crispy.

Thick-crust Pepperoni Pizza

Servings: 2

Cooking Time: 10 Minutes

Ingredients:

- ➢ 10 ounces Purchased fresh pizza dough (not a prebaked crust)
- ➢ Olive oil spray
- ➢ ¼ cup Purchased pizza sauce
- ➢ 10 slices Sliced pepperoni
- ➢ ⅓ cup Purchased shredded Italian 3- or 4-cheese blend

Directions:

1. Preheat the air fryer to 400°F.

2. Generously coat the inside of a 6-inch round cake pan for a small air fryer, a 7-inch round cake pan for a medium air fryer, or an 8-inch round cake pan for a large model with olive oil spray.

3. Set the dough in the pan and press it to fill the bottom in an even, thick layer. Spread the sauce over the dough, then top with the pepperoni and cheese.

4. When the machine is at temperature, set the pan in the basket and air-fry undisturbed for 10 minutes, or until puffed, brown, and bubbling.

5. Use kitchen tongs to transfer the cake pan to a wire rack. Cool for only a minute or so. Use a spatula to loosen the pizza from the pan and lift it out and onto the rack. Continue cooling for a few minutes before cutting into wedges to serve.

Cinnamon Apple Crisps

Servings: 1

Cooking Time: 22 Minutes

Ingredients:

➢ 1 large apple

➢ ½ teaspoon ground cinnamon

➢ 2 teaspoons avocado oil or coconut oil

Directions:

1. Preheat the air fryer to 300°F.

2. Using a mandolin or knife, slice the apples to ¼-inch thickness. Pat the apples dry with a paper towel or kitchen cloth. Sprinkle the apple slices with ground cinnamon. Spray or drizzle the oil over the top of the apple slices and toss to coat.

3. Place the apple slices in the air fryer basket. To allow for even cooking, don't overlap the slices; cook in batches if necessary.

4. Cook for 20 minutes, shaking the basket every 5 minutes. After 20 minutes, increase the air fryer temperature to 330°F and cook another 2 minutes, shaking the basket every 30 seconds. Remove the apples from the basket before they get too dark.

5. Spread the chips out onto paper towels to cool completely, at least 5 minutes. Repeat with the remaining apple slices until they're all cooked.

Muffuletta Sliders

Servings: 8

Cooking Time: 7 Minutes

Ingredients:

- ¼ pound thin-sliced deli ham
- ¼ pound thin-sliced pastrami
- 4 ounces low-fat mozzarella cheese, grated or sliced thin
- 8 slider buns
- olive oil for misting
- 1 tablespoon sesame seeds
- Olive Mix
- ¼ cup sliced black olives
- ½ cup sliced green olives with pimentos
- ¼ cup chopped kalamata olives
- 1 teaspoon red wine vinegar
- ¼ teaspoon basil
- ⅛ teaspoon garlic powder

Directions:

1. In a small bowl, stir together all the Olive Mix ingredients.
2. Divide the meats and cheese into 8 equal portions. To assemble sliders, stack in this order: bottom bun, ham, pastrami, 2 tablespoons olive mix, cheese, top bun.
3. Mist tops of sliders lightly with oil. Sprinkle with sesame seeds.
4. Cooking 4 at a time, place sliders in air fryer basket and cook at 360°F for 7 minutes to melt cheese and heat through.

Grilled Cheese Sandwich

Servings: 2

Cooking Time: 5 Minutes

Ingredients:

- ➢ 4 slices bread
- ➢ 4 ounces Cheddar cheese slices
- ➢ 2 teaspoons butter or oil

Directions:

1. Lay the four cheese slices on two of the bread slices and top with the remaining two slices of bread.
2. Brush both sides with butter or oil and cut the sandwiches in rectangular halves.
3. Place in air fryer basket and cook at 390°F for 5minutes until the outside is crisp and the cheese melts.

Shrimp Toasts

Servings: 4

Cooking Time: 8 Minutes

Ingredients:

- ½ pound raw shrimp, peeled and de-veined
- 1 egg (or 2 egg whites)
- 2 scallions, plus more for garnish
- 2 teaspoons grated fresh ginger
- 1 teaspoon soy sauce
- ½ teaspoon toasted sesame oil
- 2 tablespoons chopped fresh cilantro or parsley
- 1 to 2 teaspoons sriracha sauce
- 6 slices thinly-sliced white sandwich bread (Pepperidge Farm®)
- ½ cup sesame seeds
- Thai chili sauce

Directions:

1. Combine the shrimp, egg, scallions, fresh ginger, soy sauce, sesame oil, cilantro (or parsley) and sriracha sauce in a food processor and process into a chunky paste, scraping down the sides of the food processor bowl as necessary.

2. Cut the crusts off the sandwich bread and generously spread the shrimp paste onto each slice of bread. Place the sesame seeds on a plate and invert each shrimp toast into the sesame seeds to coat, pressing down gently. Cut each slice of bread into 4 triangles.

3. Preheat the air fryer to 400°F.

4. Transfer one layer of shrimp toast triangles to the air fryer and air-fry at 400°F for 8 minutes, or until the sesame seeds are toasted on top.

5. Serve warm with a little Thai chili sauce and some sliced scallions as garnish.

Charred Shishito Peppers

Servings: 4

Cooking Time: 5 Minutes

Ingredients:

➤ 20 shishito peppers (about 6 ounces)

➤ 1 teaspoon vegetable oil

➤ coarse sea salt

➤ 1 lemon

Directions:

1. Preheat the air fryer to 390°F.

2. Toss the shishito peppers with the oil and salt. You can do this in a bowl or directly in the air fryer basket.

3. Air-fry at 390°F for 5 minutes, shaking the basket once or twice while they cook.

4. Turn the charred peppers out into a bowl. Squeeze some lemon juice over the top and season with coarse sea salt. These should be served as finger foods – pick the pepper up by the stem and eat the whole pepper, seeds and all. Watch for that surprise spicy one!

Warm And Salty Edamame

Servings: 4

Cooking Time: 10 Minutes

Ingredients:

- ➢ 1 pound Unshelled edamame
- ➢ Vegetable oil spray
- ➢ ¾ teaspoon Coarse sea salt or kosher salt

Directions:

1. Preheat the air fryer to 400°F.

2. Place the edamame in a large bowl and lightly coat them with vegetable oil spray. Toss well, spray again, and toss until they are evenly coated.

3. When the machine is at temperature, pour the edamame into the basket and air-fry, tossing the basket quite often to rearrange the edamame, for 7 minutes, or until warm and aromatic. (Air-fry for 10 minutes if the edamame were frozen and not thawed.)

4. Pour the edamame into a bowl and sprinkle the salt on top. Toss well, then set aside for a couple of minutes before serving with an empty bowl on the side for the pods.

Herbed Cheese Brittle

Servings: 4

Cooking Time: 5 Minutes

Ingredients:

- ½ cup shredded Parmesan cheese
- ½ cup shredded white cheddar cheese
- 1 tablespoon fresh chopped rosemary
- 1 teaspoon garlic powder
- 1 large egg white

Directions:

1. Preheat the air fryer to 400°F.

2. In a large bowl, mix the cheeses, rosemary, and garlic powder. Mix in the egg white. Then pour the batter into a 7-inch pan (or an air-fryer-compatible pan). Place the pan in the air fryer basket and cook for 4 to 5 minutes, or until the cheese is melted and slightly browned.

3. Remove the pan from the air fryer, and let it cool for 2 minutes. Invert the pan before the cheese brittle completely cools but is semi-hardened to allow it to easily slide out of the pan.

4. Let the pan cool another 5 minutes. Break into pieces and serve.

BEEF , PORK & LAMB RECIPES

City "chicken"

Servings: 3

Cooking Time: 10 Minutes

Ingredients:

- ➢ 1 pound Pork tenderloin, cut into 2-inch cubes
- ➢ ½ cup All-purpose flour or tapioca flour
- ➢ 1 Large egg(s)
- ➢ 1 teaspoon Dried poultry seasoning blend
- ➢ 1¼ cups Plain panko bread crumbs (gluten-free, if a concern)
- ➢ Vegetable oil spray

Directions:

1. Preheat the air fryer to 350°F .

2. Thread 3 or 4 pieces of pork on a 4-inch bamboo skewer. You'll need 2 or 3 skewers for a small batch, 3 or 4 for a medium, and up to 6 for a large batch.

3. Set up and fill three shallow soup plates or small pie plates on your counter: one for the flour; one for the egg(s), beaten with the poultry seasoning until foamy; and one for the bread crumbs.

4. Dip and roll one skewer into the flour, coating all sides of the meat. Gently shake off any excess flour, then dip and roll the skewer in the egg mixture. Let any excess egg mixture slip back into the rest, then set the skewer in the bread crumbs and roll it around, pressing gently, until the exterior surfaces of the meat are evenly coated. Generously coat the meat on the skewer with vegetable oil spray. Set aside and continue dredging, dipping, coating, and spraying the remaining skewers.

5. Set the skewers in the basket in one layer and air-fry undisturbed for 10 minutes, or until brown and crunchy.

6. Use kitchen tongs to transfer the skewers to a wire rack. Cool for a minute or two before serving.

Pesto-rubbed Veal Chops

Servings: 2

Cooking Time: 12-15 Minutes

Ingredients:

➢ ¼ cup Purchased pesto

➢ 2 10-ounce bone-in veal loin or rib chop(s)

➢ ½ teaspoon Ground black pepper

Directions:

1. Preheat the air fryer to 400°F.

2. Rub the pesto onto both sides of the veal chop(s). Sprinkle one side of the chop(s) with the ground black pepper. Set aside at room temperature as the machine comes up to temperature.

3. Set the chop(s) in the basket. If you're cooking more than one chop, leave as much air space between them as possible. Air-fry undisturbed for 12 minutes for medium-rare, or until an instant-read meat thermometer inserted into the center of a chop (without touching bone) registers 135°F (not USDA-approved). Or air-fry undisturbed for 15 minutes for medium-well, or until an instant-read meat thermometer registers 145°F (USDA-approved).

4. Use kitchen tongs to transfer the chops to a cutting board or a wire rack. Cool for 5 minutes before serving.

Pepperoni Pockets

Servings: 4

Cooking Time: 8 Minutes

Ingredients:

- 4 bread slices, 1-inch thick
- olive oil for misting
- 24 slices pepperoni (about 2 ounces)
- 1 ounce roasted red peppers, drained and patted dry
- 1 ounce Pepper Jack cheese cut into 4 slices
- pizza sauce (optional)

Directions:

1. Spray both sides of bread slices with olive oil.

2. Stand slices upright and cut a deep slit in the top to create a pocket—almost to the bottom crust but not all the way through.

3. Stuff each bread pocket with 6 slices of pepperoni, a large strip of roasted red pepper, and a slice of cheese.

4. Place bread pockets in air fryer basket, standing up. Cook at 360°F for 8 minutes, until filling is heated through and bread is lightly browned. Serve while hot as is or with pizza sauce for dipping.

Sweet Potato–crusted Pork Rib Chops

Servings: 2

Cooking Time: 14 Minutes

Ingredients:

➢ 2 Large egg white(s), well beaten

➢ 1½ cups (about 6 ounces) Crushed sweet potato chips (certified gluten-free, if a concern)

➢ 1 teaspoon Ground cinnamon

➢ 1 teaspoon Ground dried ginger

➢ 1 teaspoon Table salt (optional)

➢ 2 10-ounce, 1-inch-thick bone-in pork rib chop(s)

Directions:

1. Preheat the air fryer to 375°F .

2. Set up and fill two shallow soup plates or small pie plates on your counter: one for the beaten egg white(s); and one for the crushed chips, mixed with the cinnamon, ginger, and salt (if using).

3. Dip a chop in the egg white(s), coating it on both sides as well as the edges. Let the excess egg white slip back into the rest, then set it in the crushed chip mixture. Turn it several times, pressing gently, until evenly coated on both sides and the edges. If necessary, set the chop aside and coat the remaining chop(s).

4. Set the chop(s) in the basket with as much air space between them as possible. Air-fry undisturbed for 12 minutes, or until crunchy and browned and an instant-read meat thermometer inserted into the center of a chop (without touching bone) registers 145°F. If the machine is at 360°F, you may need to add 2 minutes to the cooking time.

5. Use kitchen tongs to transfer the chop(s) to a wire rack. Cool for 2 or 3 minutes before serving.

Pork Chops

Servings: 2

Cooking Time: 16 Minutes

Ingredients:

- ➢ 2 bone-in, centercut pork chops, 1-inch thick (10 ounces each)
- ➢ 2 teaspoons Worcestershire sauce
- ➢ salt and pepper
- ➢ cooking spray

Directions:

1. Rub the Worcestershire sauce into both sides of pork chops.
2. Season with salt and pepper to taste.
3. Spray air fryer basket with cooking spray and place the chops in basket side by side.
4. Cook at 360°F for 16 minutes or until well done. Let rest for 5minutes before serving.

Rosemary Lamb Chops

Servings: 4

Cooking Time: 6 Minutes

Ingredients:

- 8 lamb chops
- 1 tablespoon extra-virgin olive oil
- 1 teaspoon dried rosemary, crushed
- 2 cloves garlic, minced
- 1 teaspoon sea salt
- ¼ teaspoon black pepper

Directions:

1. In a large bowl, mix together the lamb chops, olive oil, rosemary, garlic, salt, and pepper. Let sit at room temperature for 10 minutes.
2. Meanwhile, preheat the air fryer to 380°F.
3. Cook the lamb chops for 3 minutes, flip them over, and cook for another 3 minutes.

Smokehouse-style Beef Ribs

Servings: 3

Cooking Time: 25 Minutes

Ingredients:

- ¼ teaspoon Mild smoked paprika
- ¼ teaspoon Garlic powder
- ¼ teaspoon Onion powder
- ¼ teaspoon Table salt
- ¼ teaspoon Ground black pepper
- 3 10- to 12-ounce beef back ribs (not beef short ribs)

Directions:

1. Preheat the air fryer to 350°F .

2. Mix the smoked paprika, garlic powder, onion powder, salt, and pepper in a small bowl until uniform. Massage and pat this mixture onto the ribs.

3. When the machine is at temperature, set the ribs in the basket in one layer, turning them on their sides if necessary, sort of like they're spooning but with at least ¼ inch air space between them. Air-fry for 25 minutes, turning once, until deep brown and sizzling.

4. Use kitchen tongs to transfer the ribs to a wire rack. Cool for 5 minutes before serving.

Baby Back Ribs

Servings: 4

Cooking Time: 36 Minutes

Ingredients:

➢ 2¼ pounds Pork baby back rib rack(s)

➢ 1 tablespoon Dried barbecue seasoning blend or rub (gluten-free, if a concern)

➢ 1 cup Water

➢ 3 tablespoons Purchased smooth barbecue sauce (gluten-free, if a concern)

Directions:

1. Preheat the air fryer to 350°F .

2. Cut the racks into 4- to 5-bone sections, about two sections for the small batch, three for the medium, and four for the large. Sprinkle both sides of these sections with the seasoning blend.

3. Pour the water into the bottom of the air-fryer drawer or into a tray placed under the rack. (The rack cannot then sit in water—adjust the amount of water for your machine.) Set the rib sections in the basket so that they're not touching. Air-fry for 30 minutes, turning once.

4. If using a tray with water, check it a couple of times to make sure it still has water in it or hasn't overflowed from the rendered fat.

5. Brush half the barbecue sauce on the exposed side of the ribs. Air-fry undisturbed for 3 minutes. Turn the racks over (but make sure they're still not touching), brush with the remaining sauce, and air-fry undisturbed for 3 minutes more, or until sizzling and brown.

6. Use kitchen tongs to transfer the racks to a cutting board. Let stand for 5 minutes, then slice between the bones to serve.

Crispy Pork Medallions With Radicchio And Endive Salad

Servings: 4   Cooking Time: 7 Minutes

Ingredients:

- 1 (8-ounce) pork tenderloin
- salt and freshly ground black pepper
- ¼ cup flour
- 2 eggs, lightly beaten
- ¾ cup cracker meal
- 1 teaspoon paprika
- 1 teaspoon dry mustard
- 1 teaspoon garlic powder
- 1 teaspoon dried thyme
- 1 teaspoon salt
- vegetable or canola oil, in spray bottle
- Vinaigrette
- ¼ cup white balsamic vinegar
- 2 tablespoons agave syrup (or honey or maple syrup)
- 1 tablespoon Dijon mustard
- juice of ½ lemon
- 2 tablespoons chopped chervil or flat-leaf parsley
- salt and freshly ground black pepper
- ½ cup extra-virgin olive oil
- Radicchio and Endive Salad
- 1 heart romaine lettuce, torn into large pieces
- ½ head radicchio, coarsely chopped
- 2 heads endive, sliced
- ½ cup cherry tomatoes, halved
- 3 ounces fresh mozzarella, diced
- salt and freshly ground black pepper

Directions:

1. Slice the pork tenderloin into 1-inch slices. Using a meat pounder, pound the pork slices into thin ½-inch medallions. Generously season the pork with salt and freshly ground black pepper on both sides.

2. Set up a dredging station using three shallow dishes. Place the flour in one dish and the beaten eggs in a second dish. Combine the cracker meal, paprika, dry mustard, garlic powder, thyme and salt in a third dish.

3. Preheat the air fryer to 400°F.

4. Dredge the pork medallions in flour first and then into the beaten egg. Let the excess egg drip off and coat both sides of the medallions with the cracker meal crumb mixture. Spray both sides of the coated medallions with vegetable or canola oil.

5. Air-fry the medallions in two batches at 400°F for 5 minutes. Once you have air-fried all the medallions, flip them all over and return the first batch of medallions back into the air fryer on top of the second batch. Air-fry at 400°F for an additional 2 minutes.

6. While the medallions are cooking, make the salad and dressing. Whisk the white balsamic vinegar, agave syrup, Dijon mustard, lemon juice, chervil, salt and pepper together in a small bowl. Whisk in the olive oil slowly until combined and thickened.

7. Combine the romaine lettuce, radicchio, endive, cherry tomatoes, and mozzarella cheese in a large salad bowl. Drizzle the dressing over the vegetables and toss to combine. Season with salt and freshly ground black pepper.

8. Serve the pork medallions warm on or beside the salad.

California Burritos

Servings: 4   Cooking Time: 17 Minutes

Ingredients:

- 1 pound sirloin steak, sliced thin
- 1 teaspoon dried oregano
- 1 teaspoon ground cumin
- ½ teaspoon garlic powder
- 16 tater tots
- ⅓ cup sour cream
- ½ lime, juiced

- 2 tablespoons hot sauce
- 1 large avocado, pitted
- 1 teaspoon salt, divided
- 4 large (8- to 10-inch) flour tortillas
- ½ cup shredded cheddar cheese or Monterey jack
- 2 tablespoons avocado oil

Directions:

1. Preheat the air fryer to 380°F.

2. Season the steak with oregano, cumin, and garlic powder. Place the steak on one side of the air fryer and the tater tots on the other side. (It's okay for them to touch, because the flavors will all come together in the burrito.) Cook for 8 minutes, toss, and cook an additional 4 to 6 minutes.

3. Meanwhile, in a small bowl, stir together the sour cream, lime juice, and hot sauce.

4. In another small bowl, mash together the avocado and season with ½ teaspoon of the salt, to taste.

5. To assemble the burrito, lay out the tortillas, equally divide the meat amongst the tortillas. Season the steak equally with the remaining ½ teaspoon salt. Then layer the mashed avocado and sour cream mixture on top. Top each tortilla with 4 tater tots and finish each with 2 tablespoons cheese. Roll up the sides and, while holding in the sides, roll up the burrito. Place the burritos in the air fryer basket and brush with avocado oil (working in batches as needed); cook for 3 minutes or until lightly golden on the outside.

Vietnamese Beef Lettuce Wraps

Servings: 4   Cooking Time: 12 Minutes

Ingredients:

- ⅓ cup low-sodium soy sauce*
- 2 teaspoons fish sauce*
- 2 teaspoons brown sugar
- 1 tablespoon chili paste
- juice of 1 lime
- 2 cloves garlic, minced
- 2 teaspoons fresh ginger, minced
- 1 pound beef sirloin
- Sauce
- ⅓ cup low-sodium soy sauce*
- juice of 2 limes
- 1 tablespoon mirin wine
- 2 teaspoons chili paste
- Serving
- 1 head butter lettuce
- ½ cup julienned carrots
- ½ cup julienned cucumber
- ½ cup sliced radishes, sliced into half moons
- 2 cups cooked rice noodles
- ⅓ cup chopped peanuts

Directions:

1. Combine the soy sauce, fish sauce, brown sugar, chili paste, lime juice, garlic and ginger in a bowl. Slice the beef into thin slices, then cut those slices in half. Add the beef to the marinade and marinate for 1 to 3 hours in the refrigerator. When you are ready to cook, remove the steak from the refrigerator and let it sit at room temperature for 30 minutes.

2. Preheat the air fryer to 400°F.

3. Transfer the beef and marinade to the air fryer basket. Air-fry at 400°F for 12 minutes, shaking the basket a few times during the cooking process.

4. While the beef is cooking, prepare a wrap-building station. Combine the soy sauce, lime juice, mirin wine and chili paste in a bowl and transfer to a little pouring vessel. Separate the lettuce leaves from the head of lettuce and put them in a serving bowl. Place the carrots, cucumber, radish, rice noodles and chopped peanuts all in separate serving bowls.

5. When the beef has finished cooking, transfer it to another serving bowl and invite your guests to build their wraps. To build the wraps, place some beef in a lettuce leaf and top with carrots, cucumbers, some rice noodles and chopped peanuts. Drizzle a little sauce over top, fold the lettuce around the ingredients and enjoy!

Apple Cornbread Stuffed Pork Loin With Apple Gravy

Servings: 4

Cooking Time: 61 Minutes

Ingredients:

- 4 strips of bacon, chopped
- 1 Granny Smith apple, peeled, cored and finely chopped
- 2 teaspoons fresh thyme leaves
- ¼ cup chopped fresh parsley
- 2 cups cubed cornbread
- ½ cup chicken stock
- salt and freshly ground black pepper
- 1 (2-pound) boneless pork loin
- kitchen twine

- Apple Gravy:
- 2 tablespoons butter
- 1 shallot, minced
- 1 Granny Smith apple, peeled, cored and finely chopped
- 3 sprigs fresh thyme
- 2 tablespoons flour
- 1 cup chicken stock
- ½ cup apple cider
- salt and freshly ground black pepper, to taste

Directions:

1. Preheat the air fryer to 400°F.

2. Add the bacon to the air fryer and air-fry for 6 minutes until crispy. While the bacon is cooking, combine the apple, fresh thyme, parsley and cornbread in a bowl and toss well. Moisten the mixture with the chicken stock and season to taste with salt and freshly ground black pepper. Add the cooked bacon to the mixture.

3. Butterfly the pork loin by holding it flat on the cutting board with one hand, while slicing into the pork loin parallel to the cutting board with the other. Slice into the longest side of the pork loin, but stop before you cut all the way through. You should then be able to open the pork loin up like a book, making it twice as wide as it was when you started. Season the inside of the pork with salt and freshly ground black pepper.

4. Spread the cornbread mixture onto the butterflied pork loin, leaving a one-inch border around the edge of the pork. Roll the pork loin up around the stuffing to enclose the stuffing, and tie the rolled pork in several places with kitchen twine or secure with toothpicks. Try to replace any stuffing that falls out of the roast as you roll it, by stuffing it into the ends of the rolled pork. Season the outside of the pork with salt and freshly ground black pepper.

5. Preheat the air fryer to 360°F.

6. Place the stuffed pork loin into the air fryer, seam side down. Air-fry the pork loin for 15 minutes at 360°F. Turn the pork loin over and air-fry for an additional 15 minutes. Turn the pork loin a quarter

turn and air-fry for an additional 15 minutes. Turn the pork loin over again to expose the fourth side, and air-fry for an additional 10 minutes. The pork loin should register 155°F on an instant read thermometer when it is finished.

7. While the pork is cooking, make the apple gravy. Preheat a saucepan over medium heat on the stovetop and melt the butter. Add the shallot, apple and thyme sprigs and sauté until the apple starts to soften and brown a little. Add the flour and stir for a minute or two. Whisk in the stock and apple cider vigorously to prevent the flour from forming lumps. Bring the mixture to a boil to thicken and season to taste with salt and pepper.

8. Transfer the pork loin to a resting plate and loosely tent with foil, letting the pork rest for at least 5 minutes before slicing and serving with the apple gravy poured over the top.

VEGETABLE SIDE DISHES RECIPES

Roasted Garlic And Thyme Tomatoes

Servings: 2

Cooking Time: 15 Minutes

Ingredients:

- ➢ 4 Roma tomatoes
- ➢ 1 tablespoon olive oil
- ➢ salt and freshly ground black pepper
- ➢ 1 clove garlic, minced
- ➢ ½ teaspoon dried thyme

Directions:

1. Preheat the air fryer to 390°F.

2. Cut the tomatoes in half and scoop out the seeds and any pithy parts with your fingers. Place the tomatoes in a bowl and toss with the olive oil, salt, pepper, garlic and thyme.

3. Transfer the tomatoes to the air fryer, cut side up. Air-fry for 15 minutes. The edges should just start to brown. Let the tomatoes cool to an edible temperature for a few minutes and then use in pastas, on top of crostini, or as an accompaniment to any poultry, meat or fish.

Moroccan-spiced Carrots

Servings: 4

Cooking Time: 30 Minutes

Ingredients:

- 1¼ pounds Baby carrots
- 2 tablespoons Butter, melted and cooled
- 1 teaspoon Mild smoked paprika
- 1 teaspoon Ground cumin
- ¾ teaspoon Ground coriander
- ¾ teaspoon Ground dried ginger
- ¼ teaspoon Ground cinnamon
- ½ teaspoon Table salt
- ¼ teaspoon Ground black pepper

Directions:

1. Preheat the air fryer to 400°F.

2. Toss the carrots, melted butter, smoked paprika, cumin, coriander, ginger, cinnamon, salt, and pepper in a large bowl until the carrots are evenly and thoroughly coated.

3. When the machine is at temperature, scrape the carrots into the basket, spreading them into as close to one layer as you can. Air-fry for 30 minutes, tossing and rearranging the carrots every 8 minutes (that is, three times), until crisp-tender and lightly browned in spots.

4. Pour the contents of the basket into a serving bowl or platter. Cool for a couple of minutes, then serve warm or at room temperature.

Asiago Broccoli

Servings: 4

Cooking Time: 14 Minutes

Ingredients:

- 1 head broccoli, cut into florets
- 1 tablespoon extra-virgin olive oil
- 1 teaspoon minced garlic
- ¼ teaspoon ground black pepper
- ¼ teaspoon salt
- ¼ cup asiago cheese

Directions:

1. Preheat the air fryer to 360°F.

2. In a medium bowl, toss the broccoli florets with the olive oil, garlic, pepper, and salt. Lightly spray the air fryer basket with olive oil spray.

3. Place the broccoli florets into the basket and cook for 7 minutes. Shake the basket and sprinkle the broccoli with cheese. Cook another 7 minutes.

4. Remove from the basket and serve warm.

Roasted Garlic

Servings: 20

Cooking Time: 40 Minutes

Ingredients:

- 20 Peeled medium garlic cloves
- 2 tablespoons, plus more Olive oil

Directions:

1. Preheat the air fryer to 400°F.

2. Set a 10-inch sheet of aluminum foil on your work surface for a small batch, a 14-inch sheet for a medium batch, or a 16-inch sheet for a large batch. Put the garlic cloves in its center in one layer without bunching the cloves together. (Spread them out a little for even cooking.) Drizzle the small batch with 1 tablespoon oil, the medium batch with 2 tablespoons, or the large one with 3 tablespoons. Fold up the sides and seal the foil into a packet.

3. When the machine is at temperature, put the packet in the basket. Air-fry for 40 minutes, or until very fragrant. The cloves inside should be golden and soft.

4. Transfer the packet to a cutting board. Cool for 5 minutes, then open and use the cloves hot. Or cool them to room temperature, set them in a small container or jar, pour in enough olive oil to cover them, seal or cover the container, and refrigerate for up to 2 weeks.

Crunchy Roasted Potatoes

Servings: 5

Cooking Time: 25 Minutes

Ingredients:

- 2 pounds Small (1- to 1½-inch-diameter) red, white, or purple potatoes
- 2 tablespoons Olive oil
- 2 teaspoons Table salt
- ¾ teaspoon Garlic powder
- ½ teaspoon Ground black pepper

Directions:

1. Preheat the air fryer to 400°F.

2. Toss the potatoes, oil, salt, garlic powder, and pepper in a large bowl until the spuds are evenly and thoroughly coated.

3. When the machine is at temperature, pour the potatoes into the basket, spreading them into an even layer (although they may be stacked on top of each other). Air-fry for 25 minutes, tossing twice, until the potatoes are tender but crunchy.

4. Pour the contents of the basket into a serving bowl. Cool for 5 minutes before serving.

Brussels Sprouts

Serving: 3

Cooking Time: 5 Minutes

Ingredients:

- ➢ 1 10-ounce package frozen brussels sprouts, thawed and halved
- ➢ 2 teaspoons olive oil
- ➢ salt and pepper

Directions:

1. Toss the brussels sprouts and olive oil together.
2. Place them in the air fryer basket and season to taste with salt and pepper.
3. Cook at 360°F for approximately 5minutes, until the edges begin to brown.

Crispy, Cheesy Leeks

Servings: 4

Cooking Time: 15 Minutes

Ingredients:

- ➤ 2 Medium leek(s), about 9 ounces each
- ➤ Olive oil spray
- ➤ ¼ cup Seasoned Italian-style dried bread crumbs (gluten-free, if a concern)
- ➤ ¼ cup (about ¾ ounce) Finely grated Parmesan cheese
- ➤ 2 tablespoons Olive oil

Directions:

1. Preheat the air fryer to 350°F .

2. Trim off the root end of the leek(s) as well as the dark green top(s), leaving about a 5-inch usable section. Split the leek section(s) in half lengthwise. Set the leek halves cut side up on your work surface. Pull out and remove in one piece the semicircles that make up the inner structure of the leek, about halfway down. Set the removed "inside" next to the outer leek "shells" on your cutting board. Generously coat them all on all sides (particularly the "bottoms") with olive oil spray.

3. Set the leeks and their insides cut side up in the basket with as much air space between them as possible. Air-fry undisturbed for 12 minutes.

4. Meanwhile, mix the bread crumbs, cheese, and olive oil in a small bowl until well combined.

5. After 12 minutes in the air fryer, sprinkle this mixture inside the leek shells and on top of the leek insides. Increase the machine's temperature to 375°F (or 380°F or 390°F, if one of these is the closest setting). Air-fry undisturbed for 3 minutes, or until the topping is lightly browned.

6. Use a nonstick-safe spatula to transfer the leeks to a serving platter. Cool for a few minutes before serving warm.

Hush Puppies

Servings: 8   Cooking Time: 11 Minutes

Ingredients:

- ½ cup Whole or low-fat milk (not fat-free)
- 1½ tablespoons Butter
- ½ cup plus 1 tablespoon, plus more All-purpose flour
- ½ cup plus 1 tablespoon Yellow cornmeal
- 2 teaspoons Granulated white sugar
- 2 teaspoons Baking powder
- ¾ teaspoon Baking soda
- ¾ teaspoon Table salt
- ¼ teaspoon Onion powder
- 3 tablespoons (or 1 medium egg, well beaten) Pasteurized egg substitute, such as Egg Beaters
- Vegetable oil spray

Directions:

1. Heat the milk and butter in a small saucepan set over medium heat just until the butter melts and the milk is steamy. Do not simmer or boil.

2. Meanwhile, whisk the flour, cornmeal, sugar, baking powder, baking soda, salt, and onion powder in a large bowl until the mixture is a uniform color.

3. Stir the hot milk mixture into the flour mixture to form a dough. Set aside to cool for 5 minutes.

4. Mix the egg substitute or egg into the dough to make a thick, smooth batter. Cover and refrigerate for at least 1 hour or up to 4 hours.

5. Preheat the air fryer to 350°F .

6. Lightly flour your clean, dry hands. Roll 2 tablespoons of the batter into a ball between your floured palms. Set aside, flour your hands again if necessary, and continue making more balls with the remaining batter.

7. Coat the balls all over with the vegetable oil spray. Line the machine's basket (or basket attachment) with a piece of parchment paper. Set the balls on the parchment paper with as much air space between them as possible. Air-fry for 9 minutes, or until lightly browned and set.

8. Use kitchen tongs to gently transfer the hush puppies to a wire rack. Cool for at least 5 minutes before serving. Or cool to room temperature, about 45 minutes, and store in a sealed container at room temperature for up to 2 days. To crisp the hush puppies again, put them in a 350°F air fryer for 2 minutes. (There's no need for parchment paper in the machine during reheating.)

Fried Green Tomatoes With Sriracha Mayo

Servings: 4

Cooking Time: 12 Minutes

Ingredients:

- 3 green tomatoes
- salt and freshly ground black pepper
- ⅓ cup all-purpose flour*
- 2 eggs
- ½ cup buttermilk
- 1 cup panko breadcrumbs*
- 1 cup cornmeal
- olive oil, in a spray bottle
- fresh thyme sprigs or chopped fresh chives
- Sriracha Mayo
- ½ cup mayonnaise
- 1 to 2 tablespoons sriracha hot sauce
- 1 tablespoon milk

Directions:

1. Cut the tomatoes in ¼-inch slices. Pat them dry with a clean kitchen towel and season generously with salt and pepper.

2. Set up a dredging station using three shallow dishes. Place the flour in the first shallow dish, whisk the eggs and buttermilk together in the second dish, and combine the panko breadcrumbs and cornmeal in the third dish.

3. Preheat the air fryer to 400°F.

4. Dredge the tomato slices in flour to coat on all sides. Then dip them into the egg mixture and finally press them into the breadcrumbs to coat all sides of the tomato.

5. Spray or brush the air-fryer basket with olive oil. Transfer 3 to 4 tomato slices into the basket and spray the top with olive oil. Air-fry the tomatoes at 400°F for 8 minutes. Flip them over, spray the other side with oil and air-fry for an additional 4 minutes until golden brown.

6. While the tomatoes are cooking, make the sriracha mayo. Combine the mayonnaise, 1 tablespoon of the sriracha hot sauce and milk in a small bowl. Stir well until the mixture is smooth. Add more sriracha sauce to taste.

7. When the tomatoes are done, transfer them to a cooling rack or a platter lined with paper towels so the bottom does not get soggy. Before serving, carefully stack the all the tomatoes into air fryer and air-fry at 350°F for 1 to 2 minutes to heat them back up.

8. Serve the fried green tomatoes hot with the sriracha mayo on the side. Season one last time with salt and freshly ground black pepper and garnish with sprigs of fresh thyme or chopped fresh chives.

Creole Potato Wedges

Servings: 4

Cooking Time: 10 Minutes

Ingredients:

- 1 pound medium Yukon gold potatoes
- ½ teaspoon cayenne pepper
- ½ teaspoon thyme
- ½ teaspoon garlic powder
- ½ teaspoon salt
- ½ teaspoon smoked paprika
- 1 cup dry breadcrumbs
- oil for misting or cooking spray

Directions:

1. Wash potatoes, cut into thick wedges, and drop wedges into a bowl of water to prevent browning.

2. Mix together the cayenne pepper, thyme, garlic powder, salt, paprika, and breadcrumbs and spread on a sheet of wax paper.

3. Remove potatoes from water and, without drying them, roll in the breadcrumb mixture.

4. Spray air fryer basket with oil or cooking spray and pile potato wedges into basket. It's okay if they form more than a single layer.

5. Cook at 390°F for 8minutes. Shake basket, then continue cooking for 2 minutes longer, until coating is crisp and potato centers are soft. Total cooking time will vary, depending on thickness of potato wedges.

Stuffed Avocados

Servings: 4

Cooking Time: 8 Minutes

Ingredients:

- ➤ 1 cup frozen shoepeg corn, thawed
- ➤ 1 cup cooked black beans
- ➤ ¼ cup diced onion
- ➤ ½ teaspoon cumin
- ➤ 2 teaspoons lime juice, plus extra for serving
- ➤ salt and pepper
- ➤ 2 large avocados, split in half, pit removed

Directions:

1. Mix together the corn, beans, onion, cumin, and lime juice. Season to taste with salt and pepper.

2. Scoop out some of the flesh from center of each avocado and set aside. Divide corn mixture evenly between the cavities.

3. Set avocado halves in air fryer basket and cook at 360°F for 8 minutes, until corn mixture is hot.

4. Season the avocado flesh that you scooped out with a squirt of lime juice, salt, and pepper. Spoon it over the cooked halves.

Onion Rings

Servings: 4

Cooking Time: 12 Minutes

Ingredients:

- 1 large onion (preferably Vidalia or 1015)
- ½ cup flour, plus 2 tablespoons
- ½ teaspoon salt
- ½ cup beer, plus 2 tablespoons
- 1 cup crushed panko breadcrumbs
- oil for misting or cooking spray

Directions:

1. Peel onion, slice, and separate into rings.

2. In a large bowl, mix together the flour and salt. Add beer and stir until it stops foaming and makes a thick batter.

3. Place onion rings in batter and stir to coat.

4. Place breadcrumbs in a sealable plastic bag or container with lid.

5. Working with a few at a time, remove onion rings from batter, shaking off excess, and drop into breadcrumbs. Shake to coat, then lay out onion rings on cookie sheet or wax paper.

6. When finished, spray onion rings with oil or cooking spray and pile into air fryer basket.

7. Cook at 390°F for 5minutes. Shake basket and mist with oil. Cook 5minutes and mist again. Cook an additional 2 minutes, until golden brown and crispy.

DESSERTS AND SWEETS

Mixed Berry Hand Pies

Servings: 4   Cooking Time: 15 Minutes

Ingredients:

- ¾ cup sugar
- ½ teaspoon ground cinnamon
- 1 tablespoon cornstarch
- 1 cup blueberries
- 1 cup blackberries
- 1 cup raspberries, divided
- 1 teaspoon water
- 1 package refrigerated pie dough (or your own homemade pie dough)
- 1 egg, beaten

Directions:

1. Combine the sugar, cinnamon, and cornstarch in a small saucepan. Add the blueberries, blackberries, and ½ cup of the raspberries. Toss the berries gently to coat them evenly. Add the teaspoon of water to the saucepan and turn the stovetop on to medium-high heat, stirring occasionally. Once the berries break down, release their juice and start to simmer (about 5 minutes), simmer for another couple of minutes and then transfer the mixture to a bowl, stir in the remaining ½ cup of raspberries and let it cool.

2. Preheat the air fryer to 370°F.

3. Cut the pie dough into four 5-inch circles and four 6-inch circles.

4. Spread the 6-inch circles on a flat surface. Divide the berry filling between all four circles. Brush the perimeter of the dough circles with a little water. Place the 5-inch circles on top of the filling and press the perimeter of the dough circles together to seal. Roll the edges of the bottom circle up over the top circle to make a crust around the filling. Press a fork around the crust to make decorative indentations and to seal the crust shut. Brush the pies with egg wash and sprinkle a little sugar on top. Poke a small hole in the center of each pie with a paring knife to vent the dough.

5. Air-fry two pies at a time. Brush or spray the air fryer basket with oil and place the pies into the basket. Air-fry for 9 minutes. Turn the pies over and air-fry for another 6 minutes. Serve warm or at room temperature.

Molten Chocolate Almond Cakes

Servings: 3

Cooking Time: 13 Minutes

Ingredients:

- butter and flour for the ramekins
- 4 ounces bittersweet chocolate, chopped
- ½ cup (1 stick) unsalted butter
- 2 eggs
- 2 egg yolks
- ¼ cup sugar
- ½ teaspoon pure vanilla extract, or almond extract
- 1 tablespoon all-purpose flour
- 3 tablespoons ground almonds
- 8 to 12 semisweet chocolate discs (or 4 chunks of chocolate)
- cocoa powder or powdered sugar, for dusting
- toasted almonds, coarsely chopped

Directions:

1. Butter and flour three (6-ounce) ramekins. (Butter the ramekins and then coat the butter with flour by shaking it around in the ramekin and dumping out any excess.)

2. Melt the chocolate and butter together, either in the microwave or in a double boiler. In a separate bowl, beat the eggs, egg yolks and sugar together until light and smooth. Add the vanilla extract. Whisk the chocolate mixture into the egg mixture. Stir in the flour and ground almonds.

3. Preheat the air fryer to 330°F.

4. Transfer the batter carefully to the buttered ramekins, filling halfway. Place two or three chocolate discs in the center of the batter and then fill the ramekins to ½-inch below the top with the remaining batter. Place the ramekins into the air fryer basket and air-fry at 330°F for 13 minutes. The sides of the cake should be set, but the centers should be slightly soft. Remove the ramekins from the air fryer and let the cakes sit for 5 minutes. (If you'd like the cake a little less molten, air-fry for 14 minutes and let the cakes sit for 4 minutes.)

5. Run a butter knife around the edge of the ramekins and invert the cakes onto a plate. Lift the ramekin off the plate slowly and carefully so that the cake doesn't break. Dust with cocoa powder or powdered sugar and serve with a scoop of ice cream and some coarsely chopped toasted almonds.

Honey-roasted Mixed Nuts

Servings: 8

Cooking Time: 15 Minutes

Ingredients:

- ½ cup raw, shelled pistachios
- ½ cup raw almonds
- 1 cup raw walnuts
- 2 tablespoons filtered water
- 2 tablespoons honey
- 1 tablespoon vegetable oil
- 2 tablespoons sugar
- ½ teaspoon salt

Directions:

1. Preheat the air fryer to 300°F.

2. Lightly spray an air-fryer-safe pan with olive oil; then place the pistachios, almonds, and walnuts inside the pan and place the pan inside the air fryer basket.

3. Cook for 15 minutes, shaking the basket every 5 minutes to rotate the nuts.

4. While the nuts are roasting, boil the water in a small pan and stir in the honey and oil. Continue to stir while cooking until the water begins to evaporate and a thick sauce is formed. Note: The sauce should stick to the back of a wooden spoon when mixed. Turn off the heat.

5. Remove the nuts from the air fryer (cooking should have just completed) and spoon the nuts into the stovetop pan. Use a spatula to coat the nuts with the honey syrup.

6. Line a baking sheet with parchment paper and spoon the nuts onto the sheet. Lightly sprinkle the sugar and salt over the nuts and let cool in the refrigerator for at least 2 hours.

7. When the honey and sugar have hardened, store the nuts in an airtight container in the refrigerator.

Hasselback Apple Crisp

Servings: 4

Cooking Time: 20 Minutes

Ingredients:

- 2 large Gala apples, peeled, cored and cut in half
- ¼ cup butter, melted
- ½ teaspoon ground cinnamon
- 2 tablespoons sugar
- Topping
- 3 tablespoons butter, melted
- 2 tablespoons brown sugar
- ¼ cup chopped pecans
- 2 tablespoons rolled oats*
- 1 tablespoon flour*
- vanilla ice cream
- caramel sauce

Directions:

1. Place the apples cut side down on a cutting board. Slicing from stem end to blossom end, make 8 to 10 slits down the apple halves but only slice three quarters of the way through the apple, not all the way through to the cutting board.

2. Preheat the air fryer to 330°F and pour a little water into the bottom of the air fryer drawer. (This will help prevent the grease that drips into the bottom drawer from burning and smoking.)

3. Transfer the apples to the air fryer basket, flat side down. Combine ¼ cup of melted butter, cinnamon and sugar in a small bowl. Brush this butter mixture onto the apples and air-fry at 330°F for 15 minutes. Baste the apples several times with the butter mixture during the cooking process.

4. While the apples are air-frying, make the filling. Combine 3 tablespoons of melted butter with the brown sugar, pecans, rolled oats and flour in a bowl. Stir with a fork until the mixture resembles small crumbles.

5. When the timer on the air fryer is up, spoon the topping down the center of the apples. Air-fry at 330°F for an additional 5 minutes.

6. Transfer the apples to a serving plate and serve with vanilla ice cream and caramel sauce.

Brownies After Dark

Servings: 4

Cooking Time: 13 Minutes

Ingredients:

- 1 egg
- ½ cup granulated sugar
- ¼ teaspoon salt
- ½ teaspoon vanilla
- ¼ cup butter, melted
- ¼ cup flour, plus 2 tablespoons
- ¼ cup cocoa
- cooking spray
- Optional
- vanilla ice cream
- caramel sauce
- whipped cream

Directions:

1. Beat together egg, sugar, salt, and vanilla until light.
2. Add melted butter and mix well.
3. Stir in flour and cocoa.
4. Spray 6 x 6-inch baking pan lightly with cooking spray.
5. Spread batter in pan and cook at 330°F for 13 minutes. Cool and cut into 4 large squares or 16 small brownie bites.

Sweet Potato Donut Holes

Servings: 18

Cooking Time: 4 Minutes Per Batch

Ingredients:

- 1 cup flour
- ⅓ cup sugar
- ¼ teaspoon baking soda
- 1 teaspoon baking powder
- ⅛ teaspoon salt
- ½ cup cooked mashed purple sweet potatoes
- 1 egg, beaten
- 2 tablespoons butter, melted
- 1 teaspoon pure vanilla extract
- oil for misting or cooking spray

Directions:

1. Preheat air fryer to 390°F.
2. In a large bowl, stir together the flour, sugar, baking soda, baking powder, and salt.
3. In a separate bowl, combine the potatoes, egg, butter, and vanilla and mix well.
4. Add potato mixture to dry ingredients and stir into a soft dough.
5. Shape dough into 1½-inch balls. Mist lightly with oil or cooking spray.
6. Place 9 donut holes in air fryer basket, leaving a little space in between. Cook for 4 minutes, until done in center and lightly browned outside.
7. Repeat step 6 to cook remaining donut holes.

Banana Bread Cake

Servings: 6

Cooking Time: 18-22 Minutes

Ingredients:

- ¾ cup plus 2 tablespoons All-purpose flour
- ½ teaspoon Baking powder
- ¼ teaspoon Baking soda
- ¼ teaspoon Table salt
- 4 tablespoons (¼ cup/½ stick) Butter, at room temperature
- ½ cup Granulated white sugar
- 2 Small ripe bananas, peeled
- 5 tablespoons Pasteurized egg substitute, such as Egg Beaters
- ¼ cup Buttermilk
- ¾ teaspoon Vanilla extract
- Baking spray (see here)

Directions:

1. Preheat the air fryer to 325°F (or 330°F, if that's the closest setting).

2. Mix the flour, baking powder, baking soda, and salt in a small bowl until well combined.

3. Using an electric hand mixer at medium speed, beat the butter and sugar in a medium bowl until creamy and smooth, about 3 minutes, occasionally scraping down the inside of the bowl.

4. Beat in the bananas until smooth. Then beat in egg substitute or egg, buttermilk, and vanilla until uniform. (The batter may look curdled at this stage. The flour mixture will smooth it out.) Add the flour mixture and beat at low speed until smooth and creamy.

5. Use the baking spray to generously coat the inside of a 6-inch round cake pan for a small batch, a 7-inch round cake pan for a medium batch, or an 8-inch round cake pan for a large batch. Scrape and spread the batter into the pan, smoothing the batter out to an even layer.

6. Set the pan in the basket and air-fry for 18 minutes for a 6-inch layer, 20 minutes for a 7-inch layer, or 22 minutes for an 8-inch layer, or until the cake is well browned and set even if there's a little soft give right at the center. Start checking it at the 16-minute mark to know where you are.

7. Use hot pads or silicone baking mitts to transfer the cake pan to a wire rack. To unmold, set a cutting board over the baking pan and invert both the board and the pan. Lift the still-warm pan off the cake layer. Set the wire rack on top of that layer and invert all of it with the cutting board so that the cake layer is now right side up on the wire rack. Remove the cutting board and continue cooling the cake for at least 10 minutes or to room temperature, about 40 minutes, before slicing into wedges.

Chewy Coconut Cake

Servings: 6

Cooking Time: 18-22 Minutes

Ingredients:

- ¾ cup plus 2½ tablespoons All-purpose flour
- ¾ teaspoon Baking powder
- ⅛ teaspoon Table salt
- 7½ tablespoons (1 stick minus ½ tablespoon) Butter, at room temperature
- ⅓ cup plus 1 tablespoon Granulated white sugar
- 5 tablespoons Packed light brown sugar
- 5 tablespoons Pasteurized egg substitute, such as Egg Beaters
- 2 teaspoons Vanilla extract
- ½ cup Unsweetened shredded coconut (see here)
- Baking spray

Directions:

1. Preheat the air fryer to 325°F (or 330°F, if that's the closest setting).

2. Mix the flour, baking powder, and salt in a small bowl until well combined.

3. Using an electric hand mixer at medium speed , beat the butter, granulated white sugar, and brown sugar in a medium bowl until creamy and smooth, about 3 minutes, occasionally scraping down the inside of the bowl. Beat in the egg substitute or egg and vanilla until smooth.

4. Scrape down and remove the beaters. Fold in the flour mixture with a rubber spatula just until all the flour is moistened. Fold in the coconut until the mixture is a uniform color.

5. Use the baking spray to generously coat the inside of a 6-inch round cake pan for a small batch, a 7-inch round cake pan for a medium batch, or an 8-inch round cake pan for a large batch. Scrape and spread the batter into the pan, smoothing the batter out to an even layer.

6. Set the pan in the basket and air-fry for 18 minutes for a 6-inch layer, 20 minutes for a 7-inch layer, or 22 minutes for an 8-inch layer, or until the cake is well browned and set even if there's a little soft give right at the center. Start checking it at the 16-minute mark to know where you are.

7. Use hot pads or silicone baking mitts to transfer the cake pan to a wire rack. Cool for at least 1 hour or up to 4 hours. Use a nonstick-safe knife to slice the cake into wedges right in the pan, lifting them out one by one.

Peach Cobbler

Servings: 4

Cooking Time: 12 Minutes

Ingredients:

- 16 ounces frozen peaches, thawed, with juice (do not drain)
- 6 tablespoons sugar
- 1 tablespoon cornstarch
- 1 tablespoon water
- Crust
- ½ cup flour
- ¼ teaspoon salt
- 3 tablespoons butter
- 1½ tablespoons cold water
- ¼ teaspoon sugar

Directions:

1. Place peaches, including juice, and sugar in air fryer baking pan. Stir to mix well.

2. In a small cup, dissolve cornstarch in the water. Stir into peaches.

3. In a medium bowl, combine the flour and salt. Cut in butter using knives or a pastry blender. Stir in the cold water to make a stiff dough.

4. On a floured board or wax paper, pat dough into a square or circle slightly smaller than your air fryer baking pan. Cut diagonally into 4 pieces.

5. Place dough pieces on top of peaches, leaving a tiny bit of space between the edges. Sprinkle very lightly with sugar, no more than about ¼ teaspoon.

6. Cook at 360°F for 12 minutes, until fruit bubbles and crust browns.

Coconut Crusted Bananas With Pineapple Sauce

Servings: 4

Cooking Time: 5 Minutes

Ingredients:

➢ Pineapple Sauce

➢ 1½ cups puréed fresh pineapple

➢ 2 tablespoons sugar

➢ juice of 1 lemon

➢ ¼ teaspoon ground cinnamon

➢ 3 firm bananas

➢ ¼ cup sweetened condensed milk

➢ 1¼ cups shredded coconut

➢ ⅓ cup crushed graham crackers (crumbs)*

➢ vegetable or canola oil, in a spray bottle

➢ vanilla frozen yogurt or ice cream

Directions:

1. Make the pineapple sauce by combining the pineapple, sugar, lemon juice and cinnamon in a saucepan. Simmer the mixture on the stovetop for 20 minutes, and then set it aside.

2. Slice the bananas diagonally into ½-inch thick slices and place them in a bowl. Pour the sweetened condensed milk into the bowl and toss the bananas gently to coat. Combine the coconut and graham cracker crumbs together in a shallow dish. Remove the banana slices from the condensed milk and let any excess milk drip off. Dip the banana slices in the coconut and crumb mixture to coat both sides. Spray the coated slices with oil.

3. Preheat the air fryer to 400°F.

4. Grease the bottom of the air fryer basket with a little oil. Air-fry the bananas in batches at 400°F for 5 minutes, turning them over halfway through the cooking time. Air-fry until the bananas are golden brown on both sides.

5. Serve warm over vanilla frozen yogurt with some of the pineapple sauce spooned over top.

Easy Churros

Servings: 12

Cooking Time: 10 Minutes

Ingredients:

- ½ cup Water
- 4 tablespoons (¼ cup/½ stick) Butter
- ¼ teaspoon Table salt
- ½ cup All-purpose flour
- 2 Large egg(s)
- ¼ cup Granulated white sugar
- 2 teaspoons Ground cinnamon

Directions:

1. Bring the water, butter, and salt to a boil in a small saucepan set over high heat, stirring occasionally.

2. When the butter has fully melted, reduce the heat to medium and stir in the flour to form a dough. Continue cooking, stirring constantly, to dry out the dough until it coats the bottom and sides of the pan with a film, even a crust. Remove the pan from the heat, scrape the dough into a bowl, and cool for 15 minutes.

3. Using an electric hand mixer at medium speed, beat in the egg, or eggs one at a time, until the dough is smooth and firm enough to hold its shape.

4. Mix the sugar and cinnamon in a small bowl. Scoop up 1 tablespoon of the dough and roll it in the sugar mixture to form a small, coated tube about ½ inch in diameter and 2 inches long. Set it aside and make 5 more tubes for the small batch or 11 more for the large one.

5. Set the tubes on a plate and freeze for 20 minutes. Meanwhile, Preheat the air fryer to 375°F .

6. Set 3 frozen tubes in the basket for a small batch or 6 for a large one with as much air space between them as possible. Air-fry undisturbed for 10 minutes, or until puffed, brown, and set.

7. Use kitchen tongs to transfer the churros to a wire rack to cool for at least 5 minutes. Meanwhile, air-fry and cool the second batch of churros in the same way.

Fried Cannoli Wontons

Servings: 10

Cooking Time: 8 Minutes

Ingredients:

- 8 ounces Neufchâtel cream cheese
- ¼ cup powdered sugar
- 1 teaspoon vanilla extract
- ¼ teaspoon salt
- ¼ cup mini chocolate chips
- 2 tablespoons chopped pecans (optional)
- 20 wonton wrappers
- ¼ cup filtered water

Directions:

1. Preheat the air fryer to 370°F.

2. In a large bowl, use a hand mixer to combine the cream cheese with the powdered sugar, vanilla, and salt. Fold in the chocolate chips and pecans. Set aside.

3. Lay the wonton wrappers out on a flat, smooth surface and place a bowl with the filtered water next to them.

4. Use a teaspoon to evenly divide the cream cheese mixture among the 20 wonton wrappers, placing the batter in the center of the wontons.

5. Wet the tip of your index finger, and gently moisten the outer edges of the wrapper. Then fold each wrapper until it creates a secure pocket.

6. Liberally spray the air fryer basket with olive oil mist.

7. Place the wontons into the basket, and cook for 5 to 8 minutes. When the outer edges begin to brown, remove the wontons from the air fryer basket. Repeat cooking with remaining wontons.

8. Serve warm.

VEGETARIANS RECIPES

Veggie Fried Rice

Servings: 4

Cooking Time: 25 Minutes

Ingredients:

- 1 cup cooked brown rice
- ⅓ cup chopped onion
- ½ cup chopped carrots
- ½ cup chopped bell peppers
- ½ cup chopped broccoli florets
- 3 tablespoons low-sodium soy sauce
- 1 tablespoon sesame oil
- 1 teaspoon ground ginger
- 1 teaspoon ground garlic powder
- ½ teaspoon black pepper
- ⅛ teaspoon salt
- 2 large eggs

Directions:

1. Preheat the air fryer to 370°F.
2. In a large bowl, mix together the brown rice, onions, carrots, bell pepper, and broccoli.
3. In a small bowl, whisk together the soy sauce, sesame oil, ginger, garlic powder, pepper, salt, and eggs.
4. Pour the egg mixture into the rice and vegetable mixture and mix together.
5. Liberally spray a 7-inch springform pan (or compatible air fryer dish) with olive oil. Add the rice mixture to the pan and cover with aluminum foil.
6. Place a metal trivet into the air fryer basket and set the pan on top. Cook for 15 minutes. Carefully remove the pan from basket, discard the foil, and mix the rice. Return the rice to the air fryer basket, turning down the temperature to 350°F and cooking another 10 minutes.
7. Remove and let cool 5 minutes. Serve warm.

Spaghetti Squash And Kale Fritters With Pomodoro Sauce

Servings: 3   Cooking Time: 45 Minutes

Ingredients:

- 1½-pound spaghetti squash (about half a large or a whole small squash)
- olive oil
- ½ onion, diced
- ½ red bell pepper, diced
- 2 cloves garlic, minced
- 4 cups coarsely chopped kale
- salt and freshly ground black pepper
- 1 egg
- ⅓ cup breadcrumbs, divided*
- ⅓ cup grated Parmesan cheese
- ½ teaspoon dried rubbed sage
- pinch nutmeg
- Pomodoro Sauce:
- 2 tablespoons olive oil
- ½ onion, chopped
- 1 to 2 cloves garlic, minced
- 1 (28-ounce) can peeled tomatoes
- ¼ cup red wine
- 1 teaspoon Italian seasoning
- 2 tablespoons chopped fresh basil, plus more for garnish
- salt and freshly ground black pepper
- ½ teaspoon sugar (optional)

Directions:

1. Preheat the air fryer to 370°F.

2. Cut the spaghetti squash in half lengthwise and remove the seeds. Rub the inside of the squash with olive oil and season with salt and pepper. Place the squash, cut side up, into the air fryer basket and air-fry for 30 minutes, flipping the squash over halfway through the cooking process.

3. While the squash is cooking, Preheat a large sauté pan over medium heat on the stovetop. Add a little olive oil and sauté the onions for 3 minutes, until they start to soften. Add the red pepper and garlic and continue to sauté for an additional 4 minutes. Add the kale and season with salt and pepper. Cook for 2 more minutes, or until the kale is soft. Transfer the mixture to a large bowl and let it cool.

4. While the squash continues to cook, make the Pomodoro sauce. Preheat the large sauté pan again over medium heat on the stovetop. Add the olive oil and sauté the onion and garlic for 2 to 3 minutes, until the onion begins to soften. Crush the canned tomatoes with your hands and add them to the pan along with the red wine and Italian seasoning and simmer for 20 minutes. Add the basil and season to taste with salt, pepper and sugar (if using).

5. When the spaghetti squash has finished cooking, use a fork to scrape the inside flesh of the squash onto a sheet pan. Spread the squash out and let it cool.

6. Once cool, add the spaghetti squash to the kale mixture, along with the egg, breadcrumbs, Parmesan cheese, sage, nutmeg, salt and freshly ground black pepper. Stir to combine well and then divide the mixture into 6 thick portions. You can shape the portions into patties, but I prefer to keep them a little random and unique in shape. Spray or brush the fritters with olive oil.

7. Preheat the air fryer to 370°F.

8. Brush the air fryer basket with a little olive oil and transfer the fritters to the basket. Air-fry the squash and kale fritters at 370°F for 15 minutes, flipping them over halfway through the cooking process.

9. Serve the fritters warm with the Pomodoro sauce spooned over the top or pooled on your plate. Garnish with the fresh basil leaves.

Roasted Vegetable Pita Pizza

Servings: 4

Cooking Time: 20 Minutes

Ingredients:

- 1 medium red bell pepper, seeded and cut into quarters
- 1 teaspoon extra-virgin olive oil
- ⅛ teaspoon black pepper
- ⅛ teaspoon salt
- Two 6-inch whole-grain pita breads
- 6 tablespoons pesto sauce
- ¼ small red onion, thinly sliced
- ½ cup shredded part-skim mozzarella cheese

Directions:

1. Preheat the air fryer to 400°F.
2. In a small bowl, toss the bell peppers with the olive oil, pepper, and salt.
3. Place the bell peppers in the air fryer and cook for 15 minutes, shaking every 5 minutes to prevent burning.
4. Remove the peppers and set aside. Turn the air fryer temperature down to 350°F.
5. Lay the pita bread on a flat surface. Cover each with half the pesto sauce; then top with even portions of the red bell peppers and onions. Sprinkle cheese over the top. Spray the air fryer basket with olive oil mist.
6. Carefully lift the pita bread into the air fryer basket with a spatula.
7. Cook for 5 to 8 minutes, or until the outer edges begin to brown and the cheese is melted.
8. Serve warm with desired sides.

Egg Rolls

Servings: 4

Cooking Time: 8 Minutes

Ingredients:

- 1 clove garlic, minced
- 1 teaspoon sesame oil
- 1 teaspoon olive oil
- ½ cup chopped celery
- ½ cup grated carrots
- 2 green onions, chopped
- 2 ounces mushrooms, chopped
- 2 cups shredded Napa cabbage
- 1 teaspoon low-sodium soy sauce
- 1 teaspoon cornstarch
- salt
- 1 egg
- 1 tablespoon water
- 4 egg roll wraps
- olive oil for misting or cooking spray

Directions:

1. In a large skillet, sauté garlic in sesame and olive oils over medium heat for 1 minute.
2. Add celery, carrots, onions, and mushrooms to skillet. Cook 1 minute, stirring.
3. Stir in cabbage, cover, and cook for 1 minute or just until cabbage slightly wilts.
4. In a small bowl, mix soy sauce and cornstarch. Stir into vegetables to thicken. Remove from heat. Salt to taste if needed.
5. Beat together egg and water in a small bowl.
6. Divide filling into 4 portions and roll up in egg roll wraps. Brush all over with egg wash to seal.
7. Mist egg rolls very lightly with olive oil or cooking spray and place in air fryer basket.
8. Cook at 390°F for 4minutes. Turn over and cook 4 more minutes, until golden brown and crispy.

Curried Potato, Cauliflower And Pea Turnovers

Servings: 4   Cooking Time: 40 Minutes

Ingredients:

- Dough:
- 2 cups all-purpose flour
- ½ teaspoon baking powder
- 1 teaspoon salt
- freshly ground black pepper
- ¼ teaspoon dried thyme
- ¼ cup canola oil
- ½ to ⅔ cup water
- Turnover Filling:
- 1 tablespoon canola or vegetable oil
- 1 onion, finely chopped
- 1 clove garlic, minced
- 1 tablespoon grated fresh ginger
- ½ teaspoon cumin seeds
- ½ teaspoon fennel seeds
- 1 teaspoon curry powder
- 2 russet potatoes, diced
- 2 cups cauliflower florets
- ½ cup frozen peas
- 2 tablespoons chopped fresh cilantro
- salt and freshly ground black pepper
- 2 tablespoons butter, melted
- mango chutney, for serving

Directions:

1. Start by making the dough. Combine the flour, baking powder, salt, pepper and dried thyme in a mixing bowl or the bowl of a stand mixer. Drizzle in the canola oil and pinch it together with your fingers to turn the flour into a crumby mixture. Stir in the water (enough to bring the dough together). Knead the dough for 5 minutes or so until it is smooth. Add a little more water or flour as needed. Let the dough rest while you make the turnover filling.

2. Preheat a large skillet on the stovetop over medium-high heat. Add the oil and sauté the onion until it starts to become tender – about 4 minutes. Add the garlic and ginger and continue to cook for another minute. Add the dried spices and toss everything to coat. Add the potatoes and cauliflower to the skillet and pour in 1½ cups of water. Simmer everything together for 20 to 25 minutes, or until the potatoes are soft and most of the water has evaporated. If the water has evaporated and the vegetables still need more time, just add a little water and continue to simmer until everything is tender. Stir well, crushing the potatoes and cauliflower a little as you do so. Stir in the peas and cilantro, season to taste with salt and freshly ground black pepper and set aside to cool.

3. Divide the dough into 4 balls. Roll the dough balls out into ¼-inch thick circles. Divide the cooled potato filling between the dough circles, placing a mound of the filling on one side of each piece of dough, leaving an empty border around the edge of the dough. Brush the edges of the dough with a

little water and fold one edge of circle over the filling to meet the other edge of the circle, creating a half moon. Pinch the edges together with your fingers and then press the edge with the tines of a fork to decorate and seal.

4. Preheat the air fryer to 380°F.

5. Spray or brush the air fryer basket with oil. Brush the turnovers with the melted butter and place 2 turnovers into the air fryer basket. Air-fry for 15 minutes. Flip the turnovers over and air-fry for another 5 minutes. Repeat with the remaining 2 turnovers.

6. These will be very hot when they come out of the air fryer. Let them cool for at least 20 minutes before serving warm with mango chutney.

Pinto Taquitos

Servings: 4

Cooking Time: 8 Minutes

Ingredients:

- 12 corn tortillas (6- to 7-inch size)
- Filling
- ½ cup refried pinto beans
- ½ cup grated sharp Cheddar or Pepper Jack cheese
- ¼ cup corn kernels (if frozen, measure after thawing and draining)
- 2 tablespoons chopped green onion
- 2 tablespoons chopped jalapeño pepper (seeds and ribs removed before chopping)
- ½ teaspoon lime juice
- ½ teaspoon chile powder, plus extra for dusting
- ½ teaspoon cumin
- ½ teaspoon garlic powder
- oil for misting or cooking spray
- salsa, sour cream, or guacamole for dipping

Directions:

1. Mix together all filling Ingredients.

2. Warm refrigerated tortillas for easier rolling. (Wrap in damp paper towels and microwave for 30 to 60 seconds.)

3. Working with one at a time, place 1 tablespoon of filling on tortilla and roll up. Spray with oil or cooking spray and dust outside with chile powder to taste.

4. Place 6 taquitos in air fryer basket (4 on bottom layer, 2 stacked crosswise on top). Cook at 390°F for 8 minutes, until crispy and brown.

5. Repeat step 4 to cook remaining taquitos.

6. Serve plain or with salsa, sour cream, or guacamole for dipping.

Roasted Vegetable Lasagna

Servings: 6

Cooking Time: 55 Minutes

Ingredients:

- 1 zucchini, sliced
- 1 yellow squash, sliced
- 8 ounces mushrooms, sliced
- 1 red bell pepper, cut into 2-inch strips
- 1 tablespoon olive oil
- 2 cups ricotta cheese
- 2 cups grated mozzarella cheese, divided
- 1 egg
- 1 teaspoon salt
- freshly ground black pepper
- ¼ cup shredded carrots
- ½ cup chopped fresh spinach
- 8 lasagna noodles, cooked
- Béchamel Sauce:
- 3 tablespoons butter
- 3 tablespoons flour
- 2½ cups milk
- ½ cup grated Parmesan cheese
- ½ teaspoon salt
- freshly ground black pepper
- pinch of ground nutmeg

Directions:

1. Preheat the air fryer to 400°F.

2. Toss the zucchini, yellow squash, mushrooms and red pepper in a large bowl with the olive oil and season with salt and pepper. Air-fry for 10 minutes, shaking the basket once or twice while the vegetables cook.

3. While the vegetables are cooking, make the béchamel sauce and cheese filling. Melt the butter in a medium saucepan over medium-high heat on the stovetop. Add the flour and whisk, cooking for a couple of minutes. Add the milk and whisk vigorously until smooth. Bring the mixture to a boil and simmer until the sauce thickens. Stir in the Parmesan cheese and season with the salt, pepper and nutmeg. Set the sauce aside.

4. Combine the ricotta cheese, 1¼ cups of the mozzarella cheese, egg, salt and pepper in a large bowl and stir until combined. Fold in the carrots and spinach.

5. When the vegetables have finished cooking, build the lasagna. Use a baking dish that is 6 inches in diameter and 4 inches high. Cover the bottom of the baking dish with a little béchamel sauce. Top with two lasagna noodles, cut to fit the dish and overlapping each other a little. Spoon a third of the ricotta cheese mixture and then a third of the roasted veggies on top of the noodles. Pour ½ cup of béchamel sauce on top and then repeat these layers two more times: noodles – cheese mixture – vegetables – béchamel sauce. Sprinkle the remaining mozzarella cheese over the top. Cover the dish with aluminum foil, tenting it loosely so the aluminum doesn't touch the cheese.

6. Lower the dish into the air fryer basket using an aluminum foil sling (fold a piece of aluminum foil into a strip about 2-inches wide by 24-inches long). Fold the ends of the aluminum foil over the top of the dish before returning the basket to the air fryer. Air-fry for 45 minutes, removing the foil for the last 2 minutes, to slightly brown the cheese on top.

7. Let the lasagna rest for at least 20 minutes to set up a little before slicing into it and serving.

Mushroom, Zucchini And Black Bean Burgers

Servings: 4   Cooking Time: 18 Minutes

Ingredients:

- 1 cup diced zucchini, (about ½ medium zucchini)
- 1 tablespoon olive oil
- salt and freshly ground black pepper
- 1 cup chopped brown mushrooms (about 3 ounces)
- 1 small clove garlic
- 1 (15-ounce) can black beans, drained and rinsed
- 1 teaspoon lemon zest
- 1 tablespoon chopped fresh cilantro
- ½ cup plain breadcrumbs
- 1 egg, beaten
- ½ teaspoon salt
- freshly ground black pepper
- whole-wheat pita bread, burger buns or brioche buns
- mayonnaise, tomato, avocado and lettuce, for serving

Directions:

1. Preheat the air fryer to 400°F.

2. Toss the zucchini with the olive oil, season with salt and freshly ground black pepper and air-fry for 6 minutes, shaking the basket once or twice while it cooks.

3. Transfer the zucchini to a food processor with the mushrooms, garlic and black beans and process until still a little chunky but broken down and pasty. Transfer the mixture to a bowl. Add the lemon zest, cilantro, breadcrumbs and egg and mix well. Season again with salt and freshly ground black pepper. Shape the mixture into four burger patties and refrigerate for at least 15 minutes.

4. Preheat the air fryer to 370°F. Transfer two of the veggie burgers to the air fryer basket and air-fry for 12 minutes, flipping the burgers gently halfway through the cooking time. Keep the burgers warm by loosely tenting them with foil while you cook the remaining two burgers. Return the first batch of burgers back into the air fryer with the second batch for the last two minutes of cooking to re-heat.

5. Serve on toasted whole-wheat pita bread, burger buns or brioche buns with some mayonnaise, tomato, avocado and lettuce.

Pizza Portobello Mushrooms

Servings: 2

Cooking Time: 18 Minutes

Ingredients:

- 2 portobello mushroom caps, gills removed (see Figure 13-1)
- 1 teaspoon extra-virgin olive oil
- ¼ cup diced onion
- 1 teaspoon minced garlic
- 1 medium zucchini, shredded
- 1 teaspoon dried oregano
- ½ teaspoon black pepper
- ¼ teaspoon salt
- ⅓ cup marinara sauce
- ¼ cup shredded part-skim mozzarella cheese
- ¼ teaspoon red pepper flakes
- 2 tablespoons Parmesan cheese
- 2 tablespoons chopped basil

Directions:

1. Preheat the air fryer to 370°F.

2. Lightly spray the mushrooms with an olive oil mist and place into the air fryer to cook for 10 minutes, cap side up.

3. Add the olive oil to a pan and sauté the onion and garlic together for about 2 to 4 minutes. Stir in the zucchini, oregano, pepper, and salt, and continue to cook. When the zucchini has cooked down (usually about 4 to 6 minutes), add in the marinara sauce. Remove from the heat and stir in the mozzarella cheese.

4. Remove the mushrooms from the air fryer basket when cooking completes. Reset the temperature to 350°F.

5. Using a spoon, carefully stuff the mushrooms with the zucchini marinara mixture.

6. Return the stuffed mushrooms to the air fryer basket and cook for 5 to 8 minutes, or until the cheese is lightly browned. You should be able to easily insert a fork into the mushrooms when they're cooked.

7. Remove the mushrooms and sprinkle the red pepper flakes, Parmesan cheese, and fresh basil over the top.

8. Serve warm.

Quinoa Burgers With Feta Cheese And Dill

Servings: 6   Cooking Time: 10 Minutes

Ingredients:

- 1 cup quinoa (red, white or multi-colored)
- 1½ cups water
- 1 teaspoon salt
- freshly ground black pepper
- 1½ cups rolled oats
- 3 eggs, lightly beaten
- ¼ cup minced white onion
- ½ cup crumbled feta cheese
- ¼ cup chopped fresh dill
- salt and freshly ground black pepper
- vegetable or canola oil, in a spray bottle
- whole-wheat hamburger buns (or gluten-free hamburger buns*)
- arugula
- tomato, sliced
- red onion, sliced
- mayonnaise

Directions:

1. Make the quinoa: Rinse the quinoa in cold water in a saucepan, swirling it with your hand until any dry husks rise to the surface. Drain the quinoa as well as you can and then put the saucepan on the stovetop to dry and toast the quinoa. Turn the heat to medium-high and shake the pan regularly until you see the quinoa moving easily and can hear the seeds moving in the pan, indicating that they are dry. Add the water, salt and pepper. Bring the liquid to a boil and then reduce the heat to low or medium-low. You should see just a few bubbles, not a boil. Cover with a lid, leaving it askew and simmer for 20 minutes. Turn the heat off and fluff the quinoa with a fork. If there's any liquid left in the bottom of the pot, place it back on the burner for another 3 minutes or so. Spread the cooked quinoa out on a sheet pan to cool.

2. Combine the room temperature quinoa in a large bowl with the oats, eggs, onion, cheese and dill. Season with salt and pepper and mix well (remember that feta cheese is salty). Shape the mixture into 6 patties with flat sides (so they fit more easily into the air fryer). Add a little water or a few more rolled oats if necessary to get the mixture to be the right consistency to make patties.

3. Preheat the air-fryer to 400°F.

4. Spray both sides of the patties generously with oil and transfer them to the air fryer basket in one layer (you will probably have to cook these burgers in batches, depending on the size of your air fryer). Air-fry each batch at 400°F for 10 minutes, flipping the burgers over halfway through the cooking time.

5. Build your burger on the whole-wheat hamburger buns with arugula, tomato, red onion and mayonnaise.

Broccoli Cheddar Stuffed Potatoes

Servings: 2

Cooking Time: 42 Minutes

Ingredients:

- 2 large russet potatoes, scrubbed
- 1 tablespoon olive oil
- salt and freshly ground black pepper
- 2 tablespoons butter
- ¼ cup sour cream
- 3 tablespoons half-and-half (or milk)
- 1¼ cups grated Cheddar cheese, divided
- ¾ teaspoon salt
- freshly ground black pepper
- 1 cup frozen baby broccoli florets, thawed and drained

Directions:

1. Preheat the air fryer to 400°F.

2. Rub the potatoes all over with olive oil and season generously with salt and freshly ground black pepper. Transfer the potatoes into the air fryer basket and air-fry for 30 minutes, turning the potatoes over halfway through the cooking process.

3. Remove the potatoes from the air fryer and let them rest for 5 minutes. Cut a large oval out of the top of both potatoes. Leaving half an inch of potato flesh around the edge of the potato, scoop the inside of the potato out and into a large bowl to prepare the potato filling. Mash the scooped potato filling with a fork and add the butter, sour cream, half-and-half, 1 cup of the grated Cheddar cheese, salt and pepper to taste. Mix well and then fold in the broccoli florets.

4. Stuff the hollowed out potato shells with the potato and broccoli mixture. Mound the filling high in the potatoes – you will have more filling than room in the potato shells.

5. Transfer the stuffed potatoes back to the air fryer basket and air-fry at 360°F for 10 minutes. Sprinkle the remaining Cheddar cheese on top of each stuffed potato, lower the heat to 330°F and air-fry for an additional minute or two to melt cheese.

Asparagus, Mushroom And Cheese Soufflés

Servings: 3   Cooking Time: 21 Minutes

Ingredients:

- butter
- grated Parmesan cheese
- 3 button mushrooms, thinly sliced
- 8 spears asparagus, sliced ½-inch long
- 1 teaspoon olive oil
- 1 tablespoon butter
- 4½ teaspoons flour

- pinch paprika
- pinch ground nutmeg
- salt and freshly ground black pepper
- ½ cup milk
- ½ cup grated Gruyère cheese or other Swiss cheese (about 2 ounces)
- 2 eggs, separated

Directions:

1. Butter three 6-ounce ramekins and dust with grated Parmesan cheese. (Butter the ramekins and then coat the butter with Parmesan by shaking it around in the ramekin and dumping out any excess.)

2. Preheat the air fryer to 400°F.

3. Toss the mushrooms and asparagus in a bowl with the olive oil. Transfer the vegetables to the air fryer and air-fry for 7 minutes, shaking the basket once or twice to redistribute the Ingredients while they cook.

4. While the vegetables are cooking, make the soufflé base. Melt the butter in a saucepan on the stovetop over medium heat. Add the flour, stir and cook for a minute or two. Add the paprika, nutmeg, salt and pepper. Whisk in the milk and bring the mixture to a simmer to thicken. Remove the pan from the heat and add the cheese, stirring to melt. Let the mixture cool for just a few minutes and then whisk the egg yolks in, one at a time. Stir in the cooked mushrooms and asparagus. Let this soufflé base cool.

5. In a separate bowl, whisk the egg whites to soft peak stage (the point at which the whites can almost stand up on the end of your whisk). Fold the whipped egg whites into the soufflé base, adding a little at a time.

6. Preheat the air fryer to 330°F.

7. Transfer the batter carefully to the buttered ramekins, leaving about ½-inch at the top. Place the ramekins into the air fryer basket and air-fry for 14 minutes. The soufflés should have risen nicely and be brown on top. Serve immediately.

FISH AND SEAFOOD RECIPES

Pecan-crusted Tilapia

Servings: 4

Cooking Time: 8 Minutes

Ingredients:

- 1 pound skinless, boneless tilapia filets
- ¼ cup butter, melted
- 1 teaspoon minced fresh or dried rosemary
- 1 cup finely chopped pecans
- 1 teaspoon sea salt
- ¼ teaspoon paprika
- 2 tablespoons chopped parsley
- 1 lemon, cut into wedges

Directions:

1. Pat the tilapia filets dry with paper towels.

2. Pour the melted butter over the filets and flip the filets to coat them completely.

3. In a medium bowl, mix together the rosemary, pecans, salt, and paprika.

4. Preheat the air fryer to 350°F.

5. Place the tilapia filets into the air fryer basket and top with the pecan coating. Cook for 6 to 8 minutes. The fish should be firm to the touch and flake easily when fully cooked.

6. Remove the fish from the air fryer. Top the fish with chopped parsley and serve with lemon wedges.

Five Spice Red Snapper With Green Onions And Orange Salsa

Servings: 2

Cooking Time: 8 Minutes

Ingredients:

- 2 oranges, peeled, segmented and chopped
- 1 tablespoon minced shallot
- 1 to 3 teaspoons minced red Jalapeño or Serrano pepper
- 1 tablespoon chopped fresh cilantro
- lime juice, to taste
- salt, to taste
- 2 (5- to 6-ounce) red snapper fillets
- ½ teaspoon Chinese five spice powder
- salt and freshly ground black pepper
- vegetable or olive oil, in a spray bottle
- 4 green onions, cut into 2-inch lengths

Directions:

1. Start by making the salsa. Cut the peel off the oranges, slicing around the oranges to expose the flesh. Segment the oranges by cutting in between the membranes of the orange. Chop the segments roughly and combine in a bowl with the shallot, Jalapeño or Serrano pepper, cilantro, lime juice and salt. Set the salsa aside.

2. Preheat the air fryer to 400°F.

3. Season the fish fillets with the five-spice powder, salt and freshly ground black pepper. Spray both sides of the fish fillets with oil. Toss the green onions with a little oil.

4. Transfer the fish to the air fryer basket and scatter the green onions around the fish. Air-fry at 400°F for 8 minutes.

5. Remove the fish from the air fryer, along with the fried green onions. Serve with white rice and a spoonful of the salsa on top.

Almond-crusted Fish

Servings: 4

Cooking Time: 10 Minutes

Ingredients:

- 4 4-ounce fish fillets
- ¾ cup breadcrumbs
- ¼ cup sliced almonds, crushed
- 2 tablespoons lemon juice
- ⅛ teaspoon cayenne
- salt and pepper
- ¾ cup flour
- 1 egg, beaten with 1 tablespoon water
- oil for misting or cooking spray

Directions:

1. Split fish fillets lengthwise down the center to create 8 pieces.
2. Mix breadcrumbs and almonds together and set aside.
3. Mix the lemon juice and cayenne together. Brush on all sides of fish.
4. Season fish to taste with salt and pepper.
5. Place the flour on a sheet of wax paper.
6. Roll fillets in flour, dip in egg wash, and roll in the crumb mixture.
7. Mist both sides of fish with oil or cooking spray.
8. Spray air fryer basket and lay fillets inside.
9. Cook at 390°F for 5minutes, turn fish over, and cook for an additional 5minutes or until fish is done and flakes easily.

Buttery Lobster Tails

Servings:4

Cooking Time: 6 Minutes

Ingredients:

- 4 6- to 8-ounce shell-on raw lobster tails
- 2 tablespoons Butter, melted and cooled
- 1 teaspoon Lemon juice
- ½ teaspoon Finely grated lemon zest
- ½ teaspoon Garlic powder
- ½ teaspoon Table salt
- ½ teaspoon Ground black pepper

Directions:

1. Preheat the air fryer to 375°F .

2. To give the tails that restaurant look, you need to butterfly the meat. To do so, place a tail on a cutting board so that the shell is convex. Use kitchen shears to cut a line down the middle of the shell from the larger end to the smaller, cutting only the shell and not the meat below, and stopping before the back fins. Pry open the shell, leaving it intact. Use your clean fingers to separate the meat from the shell's sides and bottom, keeping it attached to the shell at the back near the fins. Pull the meat up and out of the shell through the cut line, laying the meat on top of the shell and closing the shell (as well as you can) under the meat. Make two equidistant cuts down the meat from the larger end to near the smaller end, each about ¼ inch deep, for the classic restaurant look on the plate. Repeat this procedure with the remaining tail(s).

3. Stir the butter, lemon juice, zest, garlic powder, salt, and pepper in a small bowl until well combined. Brush this mixture over the lobster meat set atop the shells.

4. When the machine is at temperature, place the tails shell side down in the basket with as much air space between them as possible. Air-fry undisturbed for 6 minutes, or until the lobster meat has pink streaks over it and is firm.

5. Use kitchen tongs to transfer the tails to a wire rack. Cool for only a minute or two before serving.

Firecracker Popcorn Shrimp

Servings: 6

Cooking Time: 8 Minutes

Ingredients:

- ½ cup all-purpose flour
- 2 teaspoons ground paprika
- 1 teaspoon garlic powder
- ½ teaspoon black pepper
- ¼ teaspoon salt
- 2 eggs, whisked
- 1½ cups panko breadcrumbs
- 1 pound small shrimp, peeled and deveined

Directions:

1. Preheat the air fryer to 360°F.
2. In a medium bowl, place the flour and mix in the paprika, garlic powder, pepper, and salt.
3. In a shallow dish, place the eggs.
4. In a third dish, place the breadcrumbs.
5. Assemble the shrimp by covering them in the flour, then dipping them into the egg, and then coating them with the breadcrumbs. Repeat until all the shrimp are covered in the breading.
6. Liberally spray the metal trivet that fits in the air fryer basket with olive oil mist. Place the shrimp onto the trivet, leaving space between the shrimp to flip. Cook for 4 minutes, flip the shrimp, and cook another 4 minutes. Repeat until all the shrimp are cooked.
7. Serve warm with desired dipping sauce.

Fish And "chips"

Servings: 2

Cooking Time: 10 Minutes

Ingredients:

- ½ cup flour
- ½ teaspoon paprika
- ¼ teaspoon ground white pepper (or freshly ground black pepper)
- 1 egg
- ¼ cup mayonnaise
- 2 cups salt & vinegar kettle cooked potato chips, coarsely crushed
- 12 ounces cod
- tartar sauce
- lemon wedges

Directions:

1. Set up a dredging station. Combine the flour, paprika and pepper in a shallow dish. Combine the egg and mayonnaise in a second shallow dish. Place the crushed potato chips in a third shallow dish.

2. Cut the cod into 6 pieces. Dredge each piece of fish in the flour, then dip it into the egg mixture and then place it into the crushed potato chips. Make sure all sides of the fish are covered and pat the chips gently onto the fish so they stick well.

3. Preheat the air fryer to 370°F.

4. Place the coated fish fillets into the air fry basket. (It is ok if a couple of pieces slightly overlap or rest on top of other fillets in order to fit everything in the basket.)

5. Air-fry for 10 minutes, gently turning the fish over halfway through the cooking time.

6. Transfer the fish to a platter and serve with tartar sauce and lemon wedges.

Fish-in-chips

Servings:4

Cooking Time: 11 Minutes

Ingredients:

- 1 cup All-purpose flour or potato starch
- 2 Large egg(s), well beaten
- 1½ cups (6 ounces) Crushed plain potato chips, preferably thick-cut or ruffled (gluten-free, if a concern)
- 4 4-ounce skinless cod fillets

Directions:

1. Preheat the air fryer to 400°F.

2. Set up and fill three shallow soup plates or small pie plates on your counter: one for the flour, one for the beaten egg(s), and one for the crushed potato chips.

3. Dip a piece of cod in the flour, turning it to coat on all sides, even the ends and sides. Gently shake off any excess flour, then dip it in the beaten egg(s). Gently turn to coat it on all sides, then let any excess egg slip back into the rest. Set the fillet in the crushed potato chips and turn several times and onto all sides, pressing gently to coat the fish. Dip it back in the egg(s), coating all sides but taking care that the coating doesn't slip off; then dip it back in the potato chips for a thick, even coating. Set it aside and coat more fillets in the same way.

4. When the machine is at temperature, set the fillets in the basket with as much air space between them as possible. Air-fry undisturbed for 11 minutes, until golden brown and firm but not hard.

5. Use kitchen tongs to transfer the fillets to a wire rack. Cool for just a minute or two before serving.

Fried Oysters

Servings:12

Cooking Time: 8 Minutes

Ingredients:

- ➢ 1½ cups All-purpose flour
- ➢ 1½ cups Yellow cornmeal
- ➢ 1½ tablespoons Cajun dried seasoning blend (for a homemade blend, see here)
- ➢ 1¼ cups, plus more if needed Amber beer, pale ale, or IPA
- ➢ 12 Large shucked oysters, any liquid drained off
- ➢ Vegetable oil spray

Directions:

1. Preheat the air fryer to 400°F.

2. Whisk ⅔ cup of the flour, ½ cup of the cornmeal, and the seasoning blend in a bowl until uniform. Set aside.

3. Whisk the remaining ⅓ cup flour and the remaining ½ cup cornmeal with the beer in a second bowl, adding more beer in dribs and drabs until the mixture is the consistency of pancake batter.

4. Using a fork, dip a shucked oyster in the beer batter, coating it thoroughly. Gently shake off any excess batter, then set the oyster in the dry mixture and turn gently to coat well and evenly. Set the coated oyster on a cutting board and continue dipping and coating the remainder of the oysters.

5. Coat the oysters with vegetable oil spray, then set them in the basket with as much air space between them as possible. Air-fry undisturbed for 8 minutes, or until lightly browned and crisp.

6. Use a nonstick-safe spatula to transfer the oysters to a wire rack. Cool for a couple of minutes before serving.

Better Fish Sticks

Servings:3

Cooking Time: 8 Minutes

Ingredients:

- ¾ cup Seasoned Italian-style dried bread crumbs (gluten-free, if a concern)
- 3 tablespoons (about ½ ounce) Finely grated Parmesan cheese
- 10 ounces Skinless cod fillets, cut lengthwise into 1-inch-wide pieces
- 3 tablespoons Regular or low-fat mayonnaise (not fat-free; gluten-free, if a concern)
- Vegetable oil spray

Directions:

1. Preheat the air fryer to 400°F.

2. Mix the bread crumbs and grated Parmesan in a shallow soup bowl or a small pie plate.

3. Smear the fish fillet sticks completely with the mayonnaise, then dip them one by one in the bread-crumb mixture, turning and pressing gently to make an even and thorough coating. Coat each stick on all sides with vegetable oil spray.

4. Set the fish sticks in the basket with at least ¼ inch between them. Air-fry undisturbed for 8 minutes, or until golden brown and crisp.

5. Use a nonstick-safe spatula to gently transfer them from the basket to a wire rack. Cool for only a minute or two before serving.

Bacon-wrapped Scallops

Servings: 4

Cooking Time: 8 Minutes

Ingredients:

- ➢ 16 large scallops
- ➢ 8 bacon strips
- ➢ ½ teaspoon black pepper
- ➢ ¼ teaspoon smoked paprika

Directions:

1. Pat the scallops dry with a paper towel. Slice each of the bacon strips in half. Wrap 1 bacon strip around 1 scallop and secure with a toothpick. Repeat with the remaining scallops. Season the scallops with pepper and paprika.

2. Preheat the air fryer to 350°F.

3. Place the bacon-wrapped scallops in the air fryer basket and cook for 4 minutes, shake the basket, cook another 3 minutes, shake the basket, and cook another 1 to 3 to minutes. When the bacon is crispy, the scallops should be cooked through and slightly firm, but not rubbery. Serve immediately.

Beer-breaded Halibut Fish Tacos

Ingredients:

- 1 pound halibut, cut into 1-inch strips
- 1 cup light beer
- 1 jalapeño, minced and divided
- 1 clove garlic, minced
- ¼ teaspoon ground cumin
- ½ cup cornmeal
- ¼ cup all-purpose flour
- 1¼ teaspoons sea salt, divided
- 2 cups shredded cabbage
- 1 lime, juiced and divided
- ¼ cup Greek yogurt
- ¼ cup mayonnaise
- 1 cup grape tomatoes, quartered
- ½ cup chopped cilantro
- ¼ cup chopped onion
- 1 egg, whisked
- 8 corn tortillas

Directions:

1. In a shallow baking dish, place the fish, the beer, 1 teaspoon of the minced jalapeño, the garlic, and the cumin. Cover and refrigerate for 30 minutes.

2. Meanwhile, in a medium bowl, mix together the cornmeal, flour, and ½ teaspoon of the salt.

3. In large bowl, mix together the shredded cabbage, 1 tablespoon of the lime juice, the Greek yogurt, the mayonnaise, and ½ teaspoon of the salt.

4. In a small bowl, make the pico de gallo by mixing together the tomatoes, cilantro, onion, ¼ teaspoon of the salt, the remaining jalapeño, and the remaining lime juice.

5. Remove the fish from the refrigerator and discard the marinade. Dredge the fish in the whisked egg; then dredge the fish in the cornmeal flour mixture, until all pieces of fish have been breaded.

6. Preheat the air fryer to 350°F.

7. Place the fish in the air fryer basket and spray liberally with cooking spray. Cook for 6 minutes, flip and shake the fish, and cook another 4 minutes.

8. While the fish is cooking, heat the tortillas in a heavy skillet for 1 to 2 minutes over high heat.

9. To assemble the tacos, place the battered fish on the heated tortillas, and top with slaw and pico de gallo. Serve immediately.

Crab Cakes

Servings: 2

Cooking Time: 10 Minutes

Ingredients:

- 1 teaspoon butter
- ⅓ cup finely diced onion
- ⅓ cup finely diced celery
- ¼ cup mayonnaise
- 1 teaspoon Dijon mustard
- 1 egg
- pinch ground cayenne pepper
- 1 teaspoon salt
- freshly ground black pepper
- 16 ounces lump crabmeat
- ½ cup + 2 tablespoons panko breadcrumbs, divided

Directions:

1. Melt the butter in a skillet over medium heat. Sauté the onion and celery until it starts to soften, but not brown – about 4 minutes. Transfer the cooked vegetables to a large bowl. Add the mayonnaise, Dijon mustard, egg, cayenne pepper, salt and freshly ground black pepper to the bowl. Gently fold in the lump crabmeat and 2 tablespoons of panko breadcrumbs. Stir carefully so you don't break up all the crab pieces.

2. Preheat the air fryer to 400°F.

3. Place the remaining panko breadcrumbs in a shallow dish. Divide the crab mixture into 4 portions and shape each portion into a round patty. Dredge the crab patties in the breadcrumbs, coating both sides as well as the edges with the crumbs.

4. Air-fry the crab cakes for 5 minutes. Using a flat spatula, gently turn the cakes over and air-fry for another 5 minutes. Serve the crab cakes with tartar sauce or cocktail sauce, or dress it up with the suggestion below.

SANDWICHES AND BURGERS RECIPES

Chicken Spiedies

Servings: 3   Cooking Time: 12 Minutes

Ingredients:

- 1¼ pounds Boneless skinless chicken thighs, trimmed of any fat blobs and cut into 2-inch pieces
- 3 tablespoons Red wine vinegar
- 2 tablespoons Olive oil
- 2 tablespoons Minced fresh mint leaves
- 2 tablespoons Minced fresh parsley leaves
- 2 teaspoons Minced fresh dill fronds
- ¾ teaspoon Fennel seeds
- ¾ teaspoon Table salt
- Up to a ¼ teaspoon Red pepper flakes
- 3 Long soft rolls, such as hero, hoagie, or Italian sub rolls (gluten-free, if a concern), split open lengthwise
- 4½ tablespoons Regular or low-fat mayonnaise (not fat-free; gluten-free, if a concern)
- 1½ tablespoons Distilled white vinegar
- 1½ teaspoons Ground black pepper

Directions:

1. Mix the chicken, vinegar, oil, mint, parsley, dill, fennel seeds, salt, and red pepper flakes in a zip-closed plastic bag. Seal, gently massage the marinade ingredients into the meat, and refrigerate for at least 2 hours or up to 6 hours. (Longer than that and the meat can turn rubbery.)

2. Set the plastic bag out on the counter (to make the contents a little less frigid). Preheat the air fryer to 400°F.

3. When the machine is at temperature, use kitchen tongs to set the chicken thighs in the basket (discard any remaining marinade) and air-fry undisturbed for 6 minutes. Turn the thighs over and continue air-frying undisturbed for 6 minutes more, until well browned, cooked through, and even a little crunchy.

4. Dump the contents of the basket onto a wire rack and cool for 2 or 3 minutes. Divide the chicken evenly between the rolls. Whisk the mayonnaise, vinegar, and black pepper in a small bowl until smooth. Drizzle this sauce over the chicken pieces in the rolls.

Mexican Cheeseburgers

Servings: 4

Cooking Time: 22 Minutes

Ingredients:

- 1¼ pounds ground beef
- ¼ cup finely chopped onion
- ½ cup crushed yellow corn tortilla chips
- 1 (1.25-ounce) packet taco seasoning
- ¼ cup canned diced green chilies
- 1 egg, lightly beaten
- 4 ounces pepper jack cheese, grated
- 4 (12-inch) flour tortillas
- shredded lettuce, sour cream, guacamole, salsa (for topping)

Directions:

1. Combine the ground beef, minced onion, crushed tortilla chips, taco seasoning, green chilies, and egg in a large bowl. Mix thoroughly until combined – your hands are good tools for this. Divide the meat into four equal portions and shape each portion into an oval-shaped burger.

2. Preheat the air fryer to 370°F.

3. Air-fry the burgers for 18 minutes, turning them over halfway through the cooking time. Divide the cheese between the burgers, lower fryer to 340°F and air-fry for an additional 4 minutes to melt the cheese. (This will give you a burger that is medium-well. If you prefer your cheeseburger medium-rare, shorten the cooking time to about 15 minutes and then add the cheese and proceed with the recipe.)

4. While the burgers are cooking, warm the tortillas wrapped in aluminum foil in a 350°F oven, or in a skillet with a little oil over medium-high heat for a couple of minutes. Keep the tortillas warm until the burgers are ready.

5. To assemble the burgers, spread sour cream over three quarters of the tortillas and top each with some shredded lettuce and salsa. Place the Mexican cheeseburgers on the lettuce and top with guacamole. Fold the tortillas around the burger, starting with the bottom and then folding the sides in over the top. (A little sour cream can help hold the seam of the tortilla together.) Serve immediately.

Black Bean Veggie Burgers

Ingredients:

- 1 cup Drained and rinsed canned black beans
- ⅓ cup Pecan pieces
- ⅓ cup Rolled oats (not quick-cooking or steel-cut; gluten-free, if a concern)
- 2 tablespoons (or 1 small egg) Pasteurized egg substitute, such as Egg Beaters (gluten-free, if a concern)
- 2 teaspoons Red ketchup-like chili sauce, such as Heinz
- ¼ teaspoon Ground cumin
- ¼ teaspoon Dried oregano
- ¼ teaspoon Table salt
- ¼ teaspoon Ground black pepper
- Olive oil
- Olive oil spray

Directions:

1. Preheat the air fryer to 400°F.

2. Put the beans, pecans, oats, egg substitute or egg, chili sauce, cumin, oregano, salt, and pepper in a food processor. Cover and process to a coarse paste that will hold its shape like sugar-cookie dough, adding olive oil in 1-teaspoon increments to get the mixture to blend smoothly. The amount of olive oil is actually dependent on the internal moisture content of the beans and the oats. Figure on about 1 tablespoon (three 1-teaspoon additions) for the smaller batch, with proportional increases for the other batches. A little too much olive oil can't hurt, but a dry paste will fall apart as it cooks and a far-too-wet paste will stick to the basket.

3. Scrape down and remove the blade. Using clean, wet hands, form the paste into two 4-inch patties for the small batch, three 4-inch patties for the medium, or four 4-inch patties for the large batch, setting them one by one on a cutting board. Generously coat both sides of the patties with olive oil spray.

4. Set them in the basket in one layer. Air-fry undisturbed for 10 minutes, or until lightly browned and crisp at the edges.

5. Use a nonstick-safe spatula, and perhaps a flatware fork for balance, to transfer the burgers to a wire rack. Cool for 5 minutes before serving.

Sausage And Pepper Heros

Servings: 3

Cooking Time: 11 Minutes

Ingredients:

- ➢ 3 links (about 9 ounces total) Sweet Italian sausages (gluten-free, if a concern)
- ➢ 1½ Medium red or green bell pepper(s), stemmed, cored, and cut into ½-inch-wide strips
- ➢ 1 medium Yellow or white onion(s), peeled, halved, and sliced into thin half-moons
- ➢ 3 Long soft rolls, such as hero, hoagie, or Italian sub rolls (gluten-free, if a concern), split open lengthwise
- ➢ For garnishing Balsamic vinegar
- ➢ For garnishing Fresh basil leaves

Directions:

1. Preheat the air fryer to 400°F.

2. When the machine is at temperature, set the sausage links in the basket in one layer and air-fry undisturbed for 5 minutes.

3. Add the pepper strips and onions. Continue air-frying, tossing and rearranging everything about once every minute, for 5 minutes, or until the sausages are browned and an instant-read meat thermometer inserted into one of the links registers 160°F.

4. Use a nonstick-safe spatula and kitchen tongs to transfer the sausages and vegetables to a cutting board. Set the rolls cut side down in the basket in one layer (working in batches as necessary) and air-fry undisturbed for 1 minute, to toast the rolls a bit and warm them up. Set 1 sausage with some pepper strips and onions in each warm roll, sprinkle balsamic vinegar over the sandwich fillings, and garnish with basil leaves.

Perfect Burgers

Servings: 3

Cooking Time: 13 Minutes

Ingredients:

- 1 pound 2 ounces 90% lean ground beef
- 1½ tablespoons Worcestershire sauce (gluten-free, if a concern)
- ½ teaspoon Ground black pepper
- 3 Hamburger buns (gluten-free if a concern), split open

Directions:

1. Preheat the air fryer to 375°F .

2. Gently mix the ground beef, Worcestershire sauce, and pepper in a bowl until well combined but preserving as much of the meat's fibers as possible. Divide this mixture into two 5-inch patties for the small batch, three 5-inch patties for the medium, or four 5-inch patties for the large. Make a thumbprint indentation in the center of each patty, about halfway through the meat.

3. Set the patties in the basket in one layer with some space between them. Air-fry undisturbed for 10 minutes, or until an instant-read meat thermometer inserted into the center of a burger registers 160°F (a medium-well burger). You may need to add 2 minutes cooking time if the air fryer is at 360°F.

4. Use a nonstick-safe spatula, and perhaps a flatware fork for balance, to transfer the burgers to a cutting board. Set the buns cut side down in the basket in one layer (working in batches as necessary) and air-fry undisturbed for 1 minute, to toast a bit and warm up. Serve the burgers in the warm buns.

White Bean Veggie Burgers

Servings: 3

Cooking Time: 13 Minutes

Ingredients:

- 1⅓ cups Drained and rinsed canned white beans
- 3 tablespoons Rolled oats (not quick-cooking or steel-cut; gluten-free, if a concern)
- 3 tablespoons Chopped walnuts
- 2 teaspoons Olive oil
- 2 teaspoons Lemon juice
- 1½ teaspoons Dijon mustard (gluten-free, if a concern)
- ¾ teaspoon Dried sage leaves
- ¼ teaspoon Table salt
- Olive oil spray
- 3 Whole-wheat buns or gluten-free whole-grain buns (if a concern), split open

Directions:

1. Preheat the air fryer to 400°F.

2. Place the beans, oats, walnuts, oil, lemon juice, mustard, sage, and salt in a food processor. Cover and process to make a coarse paste that will hold its shape, about like wet sugar-cookie dough, stopping the machine to scrape down the inside of the canister at least once.

3. Scrape down and remove the blade. With clean and wet hands, form the bean paste into two 4-inch patties for the small batch, three 4-inch patties for the medium, or four 4-inch patties for the large batch. Generously coat the patties on both sides with olive oil spray.

4. Set them in the basket with some space between them and air-fry undisturbed for 12 minutes, or until lightly brown and crisp at the edges. The tops of the burgers will feel firm to the touch.

5. Use a nonstick-safe spatula, and perhaps a flatware fork for balance, to transfer the burgers to a cutting board. Set the buns cut side down in the basket in one layer (working in batches as necessary) and air-fry undisturbed for 1 minute, to toast a bit and warm up. Serve the burgers warm in the buns.

Salmon Burgers

Servings: 3

Cooking Time: 8 Minutes

Ingredients:

- 1 pound 2 ounces Skinless salmon fillet, preferably fattier Atlantic salmon
- 1½ tablespoons Minced chives or the green part of a scallion
- ½ cup Plain panko bread crumbs (gluten-free, if a concern)
- 1½ teaspoons Dijon mustard (gluten-free, if a concern)
- 1½ teaspoons Drained and rinsed capers, minced
- 1½ teaspoons Lemon juice
- ¼ teaspoon Table salt
- ¼ teaspoon Ground black pepper
- Vegetable oil spray

Directions:

1. Preheat the air fryer to 375°F .

2. Cut the salmon into pieces that will fit in a food processor. Cover and pulse until coarsely chopped. Add the chives and pulse to combine, until the fish is ground but not a paste. Scrape down and remove the blade. Scrape the salmon mixture into a bowl. Add the bread crumbs, mustard, capers, lemon juice, salt, and pepper. Stir gently until well combined.

3. Use clean and dry hands to form the mixture into two 5-inch patties for a small batch, three 5-inch patties for a medium batch, or four 5-inch patties for a large one.

4. Coat both sides of each patty with vegetable oil spray. Set them in the basket in one layer and air-fry undisturbed for 8 minutes, or until browned and an instant-read meat thermometer inserted into the center of a burger registers 145°F.

5. Use a nonstick-safe spatula, and perhaps a flatware fork for balance, to transfer the burgers to a wire rack. Cool for 2 or 3 minutes before serving.

Printed by Libri Plureos GmbH in Hamburg,
Germany